Def - 11

AGAINST RAPE

AGAINST RAPE

BY *Andra Medea*
AND *Kathleen Thompson*

FARRAR, STRAUS AND GIROUX: NEW YORK

Excerpts from this book have previously appeared in *Ms.* magazine
The material from "Rape, Fear, and the Law," which appeared in
The Chicago Guide, is copyright © 1972 by Terri Schultz. The
material from *Soul on Ice* by Eldridge Cleaver is copyright © 1968
by Eldridge Cleaver; used with permission of McGraw-Hill Book
Company.

Library of Congress Cataloging in Publication Data

Medea, Andra.
  Against rape.
  Bibliography: p.
  1. Rape—United States. 2. Rape. I. Thompson,
Kathleen, joint author. II. Title.
HV6561.M4   364.1'53   74–4099

Contents

*The authors gratefully acknowledge the help
and support of Linda Johnson, Linda Lee,
Mary O'Connell, Kate Parker, Sara Thompson,
the women who responded to our questionnaire,
and the women of Chicago Women Against Rape.*

AGAINST RAPE

Introduction

There are a number of reasons *not* to read this book: you have never been raped; you know it will never happen to you; if it did, you know you'd never be able to remember what to do or how to defend yourself; you'd rather not think about the possibility of being raped; you or someone you know has been raped, and you want to forget about it. These are precisely the reasons you *should* read this book.

Rape, and our society's attitude toward rape, affects every woman in this country. No woman, whether or not she has ever felt threatened by an actual rape, can ignore the problem. Most of us would rather avoid thinking about it, but the underlying fear and the loaded warnings of "Be careful" have always influenced us. A black man walking through certain white neighborhoods or a white man walking through certain black neighborhoods can understand the fear of unprovoked attack. It is the same fear a woman has when she walks down the street at night—any street, even her own. Women are always in someone else's territory. They must always be careful. As a reminder of this, women have to endure the little rapes, the verbal suggestions that always carry the threat of action. These "little rapes" can turn a brief walk into an ordeal; anyone who thinks they are harmless has never considered the psychological effect of constantly being annoyed and possibly having to be afraid.

We women have aspirations and the promise of freedom for a new generation, but we have the fears of our mothers and grandmothers. The cause of our fears, in fact, is even greater than in their time.

Major crimes over all were 6 percent fewer in Chicago the first five reporting periods of this year than they were for the same span in 1971.

Rape is the most rapidly increasing, according to the charts. It is up 5.8 percent over the previous reporting period this year, and up 16.5 percent over the same period last year, and up 15.1 percent on the cumulative chart.

While major crimes in Chicago were decreasing by 6 percent, rape was increasing by 16.5 percent. The article from which these statistics were taken appeared on page 54 of the Chicago *Sun-Times* on Wednesday, June 7, 1972. A story about a cut in car-insurance rates in Massachusetts made page 10. The article made no comment about the increasing rape rates, only a report of the statistics, which is hardly surprising. Rape rates have been going up so quickly and so consistently that they are no longer news. The article went on to state that from January to May, in Chicago, 622 rapes were reported. A very conservative estimate is that reported rapes represent only a third of all rapes committed. (Some estimates go as high as one out of ten.) In other words, in a five-month period in Chicago, about two thousand women were raped. To be raped has become a fairly common experience.

On college campuses there are so many rape incidents that some large schools have put anti-rape measures into effect. At one Midwestern university an escort service was established. Women then reported being raped by the men who volunteered as escorts. On another campus, a system using police whistles ran aground when it became a source of amusement for the men on campus to whistle false alarms.

Runaways, girls of fifteen, sixteen, or seventeen, frequently report that their first sexual encounter was a rape. When they turned to a man for help in finding shelter, or jobs, or food, they often found that they were first raped, then given help. It is not just the runaway who is considered fair game; many young women on a first date feel fortunate if the evening ends quietly rather than in a wrestling match or an actual rape.

There is what might be called a universal curfew on women in this country. Whenever a woman walks alone at night, whenever she

enters a bar or a movie theater, whenever she hitchhikes, she is aware
that she is violating well-established rules of conduct and, as a result,
that she faces the possibility of rape. If in one of these situations she
is raped, the man will almost always escape prosecution and the
woman will be made to feel responsible because she was somehow
"asking for it," which could mean almost anything. Although women
are expected to be attractive, if they are attractive to the wrong
person at the wrong place and time, they must take responsibility for
some stranger's actions. For women the luxury of going out for a
walk alone, of getting away for a few minutes, is almost impossible.
Every day of their lives, women learn to accept the fact that their
freedom is limited in a way that a man's is not. There is a curfew on
women in this country and it is enforced by rapists.

During a conference on rape, the view that women were "asking
for it" was discussed. One of the two men at the conference offered to
explain. He was a man of about forty, not very articulate, and his
presence at the conference had been a puzzle. But he had something
to say.

"I've talked to a lot of men. You want to know why women get
raped? It's because they got this attitude. Like, they're walking down
the street and they're too good to talk to you. You know, some of the
guys'll be hanging around the neighborhood, and this girl's walking
around with this attitude. So maybe one of the guys'll decide to do
something about it. I mean, that's why it happens to some of these
girls. Like they just got this attitude."

There wasn't a woman there who didn't know exactly what he was
talking about. They booed in unison. He was talking about the attitude that you have a right to be where you are, that you are your own
person, and that you don't have to talk to any man who bothers
you.

So apparently women are damned both ways—they seem to be
looking for it or they look too good for it, they are touchable or they
are untouchable. Either way, they are eligible for rape. Well, we can't
accept that burden. Rape is not a price we must pay for our freedom,
any more than lynching is the price blacks have to pay for theirs.

Rape, we must remember, is a crime; women are the victims of it.
Rape is *not* the just desert of any woman who dresses casually, goes
out at night, or lives alone. And women do not *cause* rape by their

growing freedom. If we want to place the blame anywhere other than on the criminal himself, we must look at the society that creates him. Rape victims have been treated as the guilty ones, the outcasts, for too long.

As a topic for television talk shows and made-for-TV movies, rape is currently in vogue. While it is good that the subject is now out in the open, many of these programs do nothing more than to further frighten women who are already afraid. Women can do something to stop rapists. That's what this book is about. And while nothing can truly be accomplished in this area until society changes its way of viewing women, the rapist should not have an open season on women until then. Women must learn to help themselves, they must learn to help each other, and they must learn how to deal with the subject so that something can be done about it.

Mere awareness of the problem will not automatically protect women from rape. For generations, women have obeyed all the rules of behavior, and still, on occasion, they have been raped. A woman could stay home all the time, never allow a man in the house, under any circumstances. If she had to go out, she could do so only during daylight hours, dressed in army fatigues, and accompanied by a large dog. In fact, some women are already living like this. If you are, the chances are fairly good that you will not be raped. But if that, or any close approximation of that, is the way you think you have to live, you ought seriously to be questioning the world around you.

There is another way. You could take a very good self-defense course and work at becoming strong, healthy, and skilled at handling yourself. You would, of course, still have to take precautions (and in what follows we will outline these precautions for you), but you wouldn't be living in mortal fear of physical violence. You could still find yourself in a situation where there is no possibility of fighting, but at least you would have the option to fight whenever it is practical or necessary. We hope that women will learn self-defense; at the same time we realize that it is not appropriate for every woman. It takes time, energy, dedication, and the will to fight, which you may not consider to be worth the amount of freedom you hope to gain. Each woman must make the choice for herself.

As important as learning how to defend yourself is learning how to cope with the idea of rape. Until it is reduced from an overwhelming, darkly evil prospect, the individual woman will not be able to deal with it. One of the reasons for the continuing increase in rapes is that too many women are too frightened by the idea of rape to do anything about it. In addition, there are the women who are convinced that they can't fight, that they are helpless. To their way of thinking, a man will naturally always overpower a woman. This defeatism undermines them until it becomes a self-fulfilling prophecy.

Our present attitudes paralyze us, they leave us unprepared and ready to fall into man-made traps, they teach us to resign ourselves when it is unnecessary, and they lead us to believe that the situation is unchangeable.

As long as we accept the stereotypes that are presented to us in everything from pulp detective stories to Oscar-winning films—that women are naturally passive, childlike, and vulnerable, and that men are naturally aggressive, brutal, and uncontrollable—the rape situation will not change. Men will see the act of rape as a way of proving themselves; women will see rape as an inevitable threat. It is, as Susan Griffin pointed out in an enlightening article, the all-American crime.

Nice girls don't get raped

CHAPTER ONE

What Is Rape?

According to Webster, rape is the "illicit carnal knowledge of a woman without her consent, effected by force, duress, intimidation, or deception as to the nature of the act." Rape is a crime against women. Rape is a deadly insult against you as a person. Rape is the deprivation of sexual self-determination. Rape is a man's fantasy, a woman's nightmare. Rape is all the hatred, contempt, and oppression of women in this society concentrated in one act.

If rape is all these things, then to talk about rape we are obviously going to have to talk about a lot of other things as well. We are going to have to talk about how men think of women in this society, how they therefore relate to them, and what they do to them. Correspondingly, we are going to have to talk about what women think about men. We are going to have to talk about what it is in our society that not only fails to prevent rape but actively, if covertly, encourages it.

Rape is not a special, isolated act. It is not an aberration, a deviation from the norms of sexual and social behavior in this country. Rape is simply at the end of the continuum of male-aggressive, female-passive patterns, and an arbitrary line has been drawn to mark it off from the rest of such relationships. That the line is superficially imposed accounts for the tremendous confusion that arises when we try to talk about rape. It accounts for the difficulty that the laws and the courts have in prosecuting a rapist. It accounts for the fact that the average person will condemn rape as a crime equivalent to murder, but will have little sympathy for the actual victim of a rape and, as juror, will acquit the rapist nine times out of ten. We muddle around trying to draw artificial lines in the actual behavior of real persons, and we find that it cannot be done. If it happens in an alley, it's rape; if it happens in bed, it's love. If the man is a stranger, it's rape; if he's your date, it's love. If he hits you full in the face, it's rape; if he merely overpowers you, it's love.

Obviously, that sort of distinction won't work. It's the kind of distinction, however, that is drawn by the law and therefore accepted by most people in our society. Oddly, the fact that rape is sometimes prosecutable makes it difficult for most people to define, perhaps because the word "rape" is used to mean two things. Rape is always a crime, but it is not always prosecutable. This same subtlety is recognized in other crimes. Killing is not always prosecutable as murder. Hitting someone is not always prosecutable as assault. Taking another person's property is not always prosecutable as robbery. And yet, killing and hitting are seen as real acts of aggression by one person against another, regardless of whether they are ever taken to court; they are acts which may provoke revenge.

Strangely, however, in the case of rape that connection—that it is an act of aggression regardless of whether or not it is prosecutable—is not made. It is not made in the mind of the rapist. Sometimes it is not made in the mind of the victim. It is seldom made in the minds of the people the victim will have to deal with after the attack. The rape for which a man may be prosecuted differs from the rape for which he may not be prosecuted only in the way it is classified by the police and the courts. The effect on the victim is the same. The motivation of the rapist is the same.

In this book, we will be talking about *all* rapes. And we will define rape in a very simple, clear-cut way. Rape is any sexual intimacy forced on one person by another. Rape differs from acceptable sexual relations in one, and only one, concrete way. One person is unwilling and is therefore forced. It would be possible, under our definition, for a woman to rape a man. We are not going to deal specifically with that possibility simply because we feel that it is so rare in comparison to the reverse situation that to deal with it at all would be to overemphasize its importance. There are reasons that it is rare and they should become clear as we go along.

We felt that we could not limit ourselves to the prosecutable crime of rape for many reasons. First, it is very rare that a rape is prosecuted. To talk about only those cases would be to narrow our investigation to an absurdity. Second, we do not recognize as valid the distinction between rape as a crime and rape as a prosecutable crime. But finally, we do not believe that rape laws were designed to protect women from rape; the prosecutable rape is made special for reasons that we consider to be insulting and degrading to women.

As Susan Griffin pointed out in her excellent article in *Ramparts,* "Rape: The All-American Crime," rape laws are property laws.

> An article in the 1952–53 *Yale Law Journal* . . . explains explicitly why the preservation of the bodies of women is important to men:
>
>> The consent standard in our society does more than protect *a significant item of social currency* for women; it fosters, and is in turn bolstered by, a masculine pride in the *exclusive possession of a sexual object.* The consent of a woman to sexual intercourse awards the man a privilege of bodily access, a personal "prize" whose *value is enhanced by sole ownership.* An additional reason for the man's condemnation of rape may be found in the threat to his status from a *decrease in the value of his sexual possession* which would result from forcible violation. [Italics ours.]

The source of this analysis is not a feminist tract: it was part of an explanation of the nature of rape laws given in the *Yale Law Journal.* Rape as a prosecutable crime is not a crime against the woman but against the man whose exclusive possession as a sexual object she is. That is why a man cannot be convicted of raping his own wife. In the rape statutes of all fifty states it is very definitely provided that rape is the forcible penetration by a man of a woman "not his wife." Since his wife is a man's sexual possession already, he cannot be convicted of rape. He would have robbed himself.

In the case of a woman who is not married, the right of access to her body is owned by her father. Any man who forces her can be prosecuted for robbing her father. However, if a woman gives her consent, the courts can determine that, while her husband or her father was in fact robbed, she was at fault; she was the thief, and not the man.

There is one further complication. If the woman is under the age of consent, she cannot be held responsible for her act of thievery. Hence, the statutory rape laws. The man who has had intercourse with a woman under the age of consent, even if it was not against her will, can be charged with rape, with robbery of the sexual privileges of a woman. Though the two robbers, man and woman, acted in collusion, the woman is not held responsible because of her age.

This way of looking at rape is abhorrent to the woman who considers herself an independent human being, belonging to herself alone. Rape is a violation of a woman's sexual *self*-determination. Unless and until it is thus treated by the law, we will not turn to the law for our definition of rape.

Of course, to define something is not really to say what it is. We have defined rape as forced sexual intimacy, which tells us something about it. But where do we turn for a clear idea of what it is and what it means? The world of established academic research tells us almost nothing. The psychologists can tell us a little about one type of rapist, the one who falls into the extreme minority that qualifies as psychotic. The sociologists supply one book (*Patterns in Forcible Rape* by Menachim Amir) studying six hundred rape cases in Philadelphia in 1958 and 1960. The criminologists offer a few articles about where and when rape is likely to occur. And that is all.

The silence surrounding rape is, can be, no accident. There is virtually nothing, except perhaps female homosexuality, about which less has been written by the great fact compilers of our time. It is a subject which no man will touch. Or perhaps we should say that no man will touch it seriously, to try to understand it.

Outside the groves of academe, however, the subject of rape is everywhere. Comedians love it. "It is impossible to rape a woman. Any woman with her skirt up can run faster than a man with his pants down." Novelists, especially "frank, realistic" novelists, thrive on it. It is almost impossible to pick up a pornographic book without encountering at least one rape scene; it combines the magic elements, sex and violence. Moreover, pornography is a record of male fantasies, and rape is perhaps the foremost male fantasy in our society. In one form or another, explicitly or more subtly, this fantasy permeates most of what is written, filmed, and sung about love and sex between men and women.

A simple—though, if you think about it, striking—example of how the rape fantasy appears in its more subtle form is a scene straight out of every old movie you've seen. The same scene appears in soap operas on television, in serious drama and films, even in Shakespeare, with only slight variations. A man and a woman are having an argument. The woman is beautiful and strong-willed; the man can be almost anyone. As the argument progresses, the woman becomes angrier. The man wavers between anger and amusement. At last she turns to walk away. The man reaches out, pulls her around and back to him. He kisses her until she stops struggling and puts her arms around his neck.

Although this is nothing more than a kiss, the pattern is there. The man subdues the woman by forcing her to submit to him sexually, and she loves it. That is the appeal of the rape fantasy. As Ruth Herschberger pointed out in a penetrating essay entitled "Is Rape a Myth?":

> When the man turns to the sensational image of rape, he learns of a sex act which, if effected with any unwilling woman, can force her to enter into a sexual relationship with him. She can be forced into a psychological intimacy with him, as his wife stubbornly is not. Thus in the dream world of gross aggression, the husband finds the same unwilling woman of his marriage situation. But in the rape victim the unwilling woman magically becomes willing, her sensory nerves respond gratefully, stubborn reflexes react obediently, and the beautiful stranger willy-nilly enters into a state of sexual intimacy with her aggressor.

The man, of course, need not be a husband: he can be any man who has been frustrated by dealing with unwilling women. In a world where all women are supposed to be unwilling, he dreams not of finding a different sort of woman who will return his fervor (that sort of woman is a slut and therefore not an appealing fantasy figure), but of overcoming a woman in spite of her unwillingness. Then, and only then, will she realize how much she wants him.

It is a perverse world which produces this fantasy. But once it is established that men are naturally aggressive while women are naturally passive, that men have strong sexual desires and that women have none, perversity is inevitable. In our society, the rape fantasy is *normal*.

It is the fantasies of rape, or perhaps we should say the myths, that have formed our ideas of rape because they are all we ever hear about it. There are two myths, separate and contradictory. One applies to the women a man would himself like to rape; the other is for the women he knows, women who fear rape—his mother, his sister, his daughter, or his wife. One is no more true than the other. In the first, as we have seen, the man overcomes the unwilling woman, who enjoys it. In the other, the rapist is not a "normal" man but some hulking, slavering maniac who drags the woman into a dark alley, beats her up, and rapes her. This woman, far from enjoying it, is driven out of her mind by the attack. No decent woman, according to this myth, could survive a rape without, at the very least, losing her sanity.

That is not the way it is, though. That is not the way rapes happen. This is the way they happen.

The woman is nineteen, a resident counselor in a girls' dorm at a coeducational university. It is about two o'clock in the afternoon and she is in an isolated part of one of the school buildings. Her attacker is a young married man who is a lecturer at the university.

The woman is seventeen, a high-school student. It is about four o'clock in the afternoon. Her boy friend's father has picked her up in his car after school to take her to meet his son. He stops by his house and says she should wait for him in the car. When he has pulled the car into the garage, this thirty-seven-year-old father of six rapes her.

The woman is thirty-nine, separated from her husband, the mother of five children. Her attacker breaks into the house in the middle of the night. He turns out to be a friend's husband, the father of several children.

The woman is twenty and has recently been hired for a new job. The boss asks her to come in on a holiday to help with the inventory. When she arrives, there is no one else there. Her boss, a man of about thirty, rapes her.

The woman is sixteen, a high-school student. She has a date with a college student she knows fairly well. He drives her to an isolated area and rapes her.

The woman is twenty-three. She is hitchhiking. A friendly man in a new red farm truck picks her up. He talks quietly and respectfully to her until he pulls off the highway, turns onto a dirt road, brings out a knife, and rapes her. It is "just part of the fun of hitchhiking," he tells her as he drives her back to the highway, "because it's a long way and I'm a nice guy."

The victims in these cases responded to a questionnaire we had printed in a number of papers. None of them "enjoyed" the rape. None of them lost her mind. None of the rapes took place in a dark alley at night. In fact, none of them fits into the standard myths about rape at all. Very few of the more than one hundred rape reports we obtained in this way shared even one characteristic with either of our two major rape myths.

It is not surprising, really, that a myth should fail to match a reality. What is surprising is that, in the case of rape, myth has for so long been served up to us as reality. In the last two years women themselves have begun to talk and write about rape, and at last some truths are being told. But we still know so little. There is so much to be said. Only when we begin to understand rape can we fight it, and fight it we must.

The brave deserve the lovely—every woman may be won.
    Charles Godfrey, *The Masher*

Rape is in this sense a mirror-image of our ordinary sex folkways. Two basic beliefs in these folkways are the natural sexual aggressiveness of man, and man's natural physical superiority over women. Put these two beliefs together, set up a competition for masculine prowess such as we have today, and no one should be surprised by the incidence of rape.
    Ruth Herschberger, *Adam's Rib*

Those men [convicted rapists] *were the most normal men there. They had a lot of hang-ups, but they were the same hang-ups as men walking out on the street.*
    Allan Taylor, parole officer at San Luis
    Obispo, California, quoted in "Rape:
    The All-American Crime," by Susan Griffin

CHAPTER TWO

Why Do Men Rape Women?

In researching this book, we relied heavily on descriptions by rape victims. From these women's experiences and from our own experiences, we were able to gain some insight into the way a rape situation works. It appears that there are two dynamics operating: hostility (including such emotions as rage, hatred, contempt, and the desire to humiliate) and gratification. A rape may be motivated entirely by one or the other, but it is much more often a combination of the two.

The rape in which hostility is the main factor is a very dangerous and frightening situation. Here sexual release is a secondary, perhaps even negligible, factor. This sort of rape is not necessarily characterized by brutality, but includes it more frequently than the other; in any case, whether actual brutality is involved or not, the act is essentially one of violence. The subjugation of the victim is basic to the rapist's satisfaction.

The second sort of rape, in which sexual gratification is the primary motivation, is more ambiguous, more confusing to the woman and to the people she turns to for help afterward. It is not likely that the rapist will go so far as to brutalize the woman to gain what he wants: the brutality itself is not particularly appealing to him. He will threaten, overpower, and blackmail, but not kill or beat her to get what he wants.

One must begin to wonder about a society that produces so many men capable of either sort of rape.

The first sort of rapist is the man who buys the John Wayne brand of masculinity. Ideally, the qualities we call masculine and the qualities we call feminine should be balanced in an individual. When they are out of balance, the result is a monster. The personality traits which have been labeled masculine include strength, independence, aggressiveness, self-control, rationality. The feminine ideal is soft, sensitive, accepting, intuitive, loving. These are all positive terms. But to see what horrors can result from an imbalance in either direction, let us use the negative terms, the words which would be used to describe the same characteristics in a member of the "wrong" sex. A woman would be hard, bullheaded, pushy, cold, and calculating if she took on "masculine" traits. A man would be weak, spineless, stupid, and a sissy if he took on "feminine" traits.

To take this one step further, we would suggest that the very masculine *man* is hard, bullheaded, pushy, cold, and calculating. He is also a potential rapist. Aggressiveness—unchecked by sensitivity, gentleness, and concern for others—is a basic trait of the rapist. Similarly, the woman who lives up, or down, to the feminine ideal *is* weak. She is unprotected against her "natural" opposite, the "aggressive male." Both are in bad shape, but it doesn't take much to figure out which one is going to be hurt. It may be restrictive to be reared to beat up other people, but there is no doubt that to be trained to be beaten up is more painful.

The result of this conditioning is that it incapacitates women for an independent existence, making them dependent on men for protection. And it makes men who buy what is essentially the code of chivalry likely *either* to protect women or to victimize them. The two impulses come from the same source, and the same men will probably do both, at different times and to different women. If this sort of man wants to vent his hostility, even a general, nonspecific hostility, he sees women as the victims authorized by society. The code of chivalry decrees that only a coward would hit a woman, but millions of men beat their wives, hit their girl friends, and, sometimes, rape strangers on the street: clearly, it is only certain women, under certain circumstances, who are protected by that code. It makes the rest of womankind more, not less, likely to be attacked. As Susan Griffin pointed out, Sir Thomas Malory, whose *Morte d'Arthur* is the most nearly perfect statement of chivalry and its glories, was repeatedly arrested for rape.

This ultramasculine male or, more usually, the man who needs to see himself that way, is trying to play a role that is not natural to any human being. In his extreme form, he must constantly be on guard against any evidence of "femininity" in himself, and so he becomes frightened of that femininity. He fears and hates women. In order to bolster his own masculinity, he expresses contempt for women. The more insecure he is, the more he exaggerates the qualities he sees as masculine—aggressiveness, brutality, violence. And when he comes closest to being what he sees as the ideal, he becomes a rapist.

The second sort of rapist differs from this pattern. He is like the first (like most men in our society) in his basic inability to see women as human beings. To the first type they are contemptible and threatening. To the second they are simply objects. Like the first sort of rape, the rape for gratification is a product of sexual conditioning in our society, but in a slightly different way. It derives directly from the patterns of sexual behavior, the courtship ritual in which a woman possesses and guards a prize which the man attempts to win from her.

This kind of rapist is the man who thinks of sex as something he has to pay for, manipulate for, work for, perhaps marry and support a family for. He has always been taught that no woman really wants to have sex and that he will have to bargain for it. The most successful man, to him and to most of our society, is the man who makes the best bargain, who pays the least for his sex.

When this man rapes, he is simply taking sex without paying for it. In his own mind he is not degrading the woman or humiliating her, he is simply getting the best of her. He does not hate her, or even especially lust after her: almost any vaguely attractive woman would suit his purpose. If he knows the woman and she lets herself be put into the situation that allows him to rape her, he will almost certainly not think that he has raped her. She has made a false move in the game and it only makes sense for him to take advantage of it. If he doesn't know her, as in the case of the man who picks up a hitch-hiker, he may realize that he has raped her, but it will not register with him as RAPE. He knows as well as everyone else what a rapist is, and he knows he isn't like that.

Perhaps the most common reason for rape is that a man sees the opportunity to have intercourse with a woman, under circumstances where she is unlikely to tell anyone about it or she is unlikely to be believed. One woman reported to us that she was raped while trying to arrange an illegal abortion. The rapist knew that she would not report him for fear that information about her abortion would come out. So he took advantage of the situation.

That is one obvious example of this sort of rape. There are many which are not so obvious. Any time a woman is in a "compromising" situation, rape is a possibility. On our questionnaires the *majority* of the women who responded that they did not know the men who raped them had been hitchhiking at the time of the rape. The fact that she is hitchhiking makes any woman fair game for this kind of man. She will probably not report him, and if she does, he will almost certainly not be prosecuted. One woman reported to us that she was able to relate her story to a captain in the police department of the city where she was raped only because a friend knew him. He listened sympathetically to her and then said that there simply was no possibility that the rapist would be prosecuted, even though he had held a knife to her throat, because she had been hitchhiking at the time and not wearing a bra.

It is outrageous, of course, that a man can rape a woman without being punished, but what is worse is that the freedom from the consequences of his action seems to be a motivation for the rapist's attack, sometimes the sole motivation. The man rapes the woman *because* he will not have to pay for his actions. That same man would be no danger to the woman who lives next door, the woman who is a friend of his wife's, the woman he works with—unless he found himself in a situation with one of them that he knew would prevent her from telling anyone.

As we said, this seems to be the most common kind of rape, and the one for which there is the least sympathy. It is marked by a lack of any feeling of guilt on the part of the rapist and an extraordinary amount of guilt on the part of the victim. And, since it arises directly from the ordinary patterns of sexual behavior in our society, that reaction is understandable. The male is the aggressor, the soldier laying siege to the castle; the woman is the guardian of the gate, the defender of the sacred treasure. If the male forces his way in with a battering ram and captures the treasure, he has succeeded in his purpose. There is no cause for guilt or remorse. The woman, on the other hand, has failed in her purpose. She has allowed the treasure to be taken and feels herself to be at fault. She suffers from feelings of guilt, besides the feelings of violation, humiliation, and defeat. And society, her family, the police, and the courts see her the same way. She has lacked the proper vigilance in guarding the treasure. Why was she hitchhiking? Why was she out so late at night? Why did she let him into her apartment? they will ask, as they would ask a sentinel why he fell asleep on guard duty. Seeing man and woman in these terms makes it impossible to deal with rape rationally. No woman who sees herself that way can be free from guilt. To be raped is to be guilty, in one's own eyes as well as in everyone else's.

Assume for the moment that both men and women have sexual desires and that both are capable either of acting on them or ignoring them (and not that men must act on their sexual desires and women must ignore theirs, if indeed they have them). Assume that a man may ask a woman if she would like to have sex with him and that a woman may do the same (and not that he will have to trick her or talk her into it, or that she will have to make coy suggestions and flirtatious gestures). Assume that the one who is asked will respond truthfully. What happens then to our perception of this common form of rape? Under these circumstances, the man who forced the woman would have to face the consequences. The woman would be outraged at the violation of her sexual self-determination instead of feeling humiliated at the loss of her treasure. Society would respond as it now responds to murder or a brutal assault, with compassion for the victim and rage at the attacker.

All of the above assumptions are at least talked about in our present sexual revolution. Some women believe that they are already true. These women act on that belief and often they find themselves caught in a trap that ends in rape. Moreover, women who believe in sexual self-determination are further shocked when they hear other people's reactions to their predicament. Again and again women told us, "The reaction of the police was, if possible, worse than the rape," or "I couldn't understand my boy friend's response when I told him.

He was angry with me for being stupid enough to get raped." These reactions often seem worse than the rape because they are so unexpected and what they imply is so terrible.

The rape victim's first reaction is usually to see the rape as a freakish accident or an isolated event and to see the rapist as a lunatic. But when the authorities and her family treat her with the same horror and contempt that should be directed at the rapist, she is forced either to question society's attitude toward rape or to begin to doubt herself. Unfortunately, the latter is what most often happens.

Perhaps the most horrible thing to deal with in these cases is the attitude of the rapist himself. However profound one's feelings of rage against him, they are unlikely to pierce his armor of indifference. He does not feel guilty for what he has done and is likely to see his victim as a raving idiot. One woman reported that her attacker called her and asked her for a date the next weekend—and was taken completely by surprise when she screamed with anger. He shrugged it off and called someone else.

In the end, the victim is likely to bury the attack in the back of her mind as a horrible, bewildering incident that she cannot cope with. And when she is asked, as we asked at rape conferences and on our questionnaires, "Have you ever been raped?" she will answer, as so many women did, "I don't know."

Man is the powder; Woman the spark.
          Lope de Vega, *La Dama Melindrosa*

Women often wish to give unwillingly what they really like to give.
          Ovid, *Ars amatoria*

A man no more believes a woman when she says she has an aversion for him than when she says she'll cry out.
          William Wycherley, *The Plain Dealer*

CHAPTER THREE

Who Is the Rapist?

We have talked about two categories of rape, or rather, two kinds of rapist. Each is the product of a certain type of male conditioning in our society. To some degree most men fall into one or both of those categories. In that sense, most men in our country are potential rapists. But, you might ask, doesn't something have to snap in a man, doesn't something have to go dreadfully wrong with his mind for him to become a rapist? Isn't the rapist really sick, a sexual deviant whose actions are universally condemned by other men and who rapes in spite of all the best efforts of society to stop him? Perhaps the potential for rape lies in all men in our society, but, you ask yourself, isn't it a potential that must be aggravated and exaggerated to the point of sickness before a man actually rapes? If you believe that, you are in for a shock. The rapist is the man next door.

If a woman is raped, according to statistics from the study by Menachim Amir and according to the results of our questionnaire, the chances are better than 50 percent that her attacker will be someone she knows. Again, according to our questionnaire, the chances are better than 50 percent that he will behave calmly and matter-of-factly. A recent study showed that convicted rapists were indistinguishable from ordinary men in psychological tests. Some of them showed a slight tendency to express anger more openly, but sexually, and in all other ways, they were average. In this they differed from other sex offenders, such as exhibitionists, who did show a significant difference from both rapists and ordinary men. With the exception of about 3 percent, rapists seem to be sexually and psychologically normal.

In "The Banality of Evil," Hannah Arendt attempted to explain the success of the Nazis in wartime Germany. Put very simply, her argument was that there are very few evil people and a lot of very ordinary people who do evil things. And that is the horror of evil, that it is not recognizable, that it is not a thing reserved for extraordinary creatures. The effect of this insight is not to make the Nazi atrocities less fearful, but more. If the men who gassed, shot, and otherwise murdered six million people, who performed inconceivably inhuman acts on their victims, were not madmen, if they were not *evil* men (as their leader Hitler surely was), then we have to come to terms with some terrible truths: first we have to recognize that the capacity for evil of that magnitude lies within the people around us, within ourselves. Then we must realize that the capacity for evil is only one part of a human being: that he will not always act, look, or be evil. A man can love animals, treat his customers fairly, be kind and loving with his family, and kill Jews. Or rape women.

Recognizing that rapists are in no significant sense different from other men does not make the act less horrible. Rather, it brings into question the society in which ordinary men *can* be rapists. Ordinary men could perform atrocities at Buchenwald and Mylai because their victims were Jews and gooks. They had been told, and they believed, that the people they were killing were not really human beings, not as they and their friends and families were human beings. This is the basis of the most horrible racial crimes. People raised in the North, hearing the stories of lynchings and castrations of blacks in the South, are often shocked when they meet their first Southern bigot. The man who participated in a lynching party last night might be the perfect baby-sitter for a two-year-old child this afternoon, if that child is white. For a racist, skin color can disqualify one as a human being, can put one into a category of creatures against whom it is permissible to act in ways that he never could against one of his own kind. And for the sexist man (and most men in our society are sexist), sex puts one into the same kind of category.

One of the women who responded to our questionnaire was the victim of a particularly brutal gang rape. After the rapists had finished with her, they took her in a car to dump somewhere. As they were driving along, they said, "Let's get rid of this one and find another piece of meat." They had not humiliated, degraded, beaten, and terrified a human being: they had used a piece of meat. If an ordinary woman is a piece of ass, a box, a lay, a cunt, a hippie chick, a whore, then the ordinary man is a rapist. The man who asks another, "Did you score? Does she put out? Had any lately?" is a potential rapist.

Some might say we are being too sensitive about language. It is not merely the language; that's a symptom. The image expressed by the phrase "piece of meat" was perfectly illustrated in a recent movie, *Prime Cut.* In the movie, a group of gangsters kept women drugged in cowpens to be sold, as meat is sold, to whorehouses. This is not an unusual example of the way women have been portrayed in movies. It is simply a particularly clear one. The same sort of image can be seen everywhere—on the runway in Atlantic City once a year, for example. It is all part of the same process of dehumanization. When you look at what human beings have done to the people whom they exclude from the human race by that sort of language—what human beings have done to niggers and kikes and chinks and broads—it is easy to see why we object. There is a set of rules governing the behavior of one human being toward another, and we want women to be recognized as human beings and given the protection of those rules. Today, in this society, women do not have that status and, among other things, they get raped.

Most people would suggest that the ordinary man only rapes if he is suddenly overcome by an uncontrollable sexual urge. That is the next part of the false myth about rape: a man is walking down the street when a provocatively attired woman causes him to attack her by her seductive behavior. The fallacy of that particular myth is easily demonstrated. In *Patterns in Forcible Rape,* Menachim Amir revealed that the majority of the rapes in his study were premeditated. Of all the rapes, single and group, 82.1 percent were wholly or partially planned in advance. This is what the statisticians call a significant majority. In fact, it is what anyone would call a significant majority. Less than one in five of the men in the study committed spontaneous rapes triggered by impulse, and some of these were of the "rape her on the way out, the rape is free" variety, committed after a burglary. That pretty well destroys the "she was asking for it" theory of rape. And, in addition, we must contradict the idea of rape as a "natural" act, a regrettable but unavoidable part of human behavior made necessary because men have overwhelming sexual desires that must find an outlet. If that were true, one would expect most rapists to be unmarried men with no other form of sexual release. They aren't. Rapists are neither permanently insane nor temporarily insane with sexual frustration.

There is plenty of support for this view. Human history is filled with rapists who have been neither sick nor overcome by lust. In warfare, for example, rape holds a time-honored place. Conquering armies attack the civilian population by murder, looting, and rape. To the victor belongs the spoils, and spoils include women. When they confiscate and destroy other property, the soldiers also rape the women. These men are not sick. They are not overcome by sexual desire.

The world recently witnessed another incident of mass rape. Army activities in Bangla Desh emphasized its use as a tactic. West Pakistanis had little money to wage war, so their soldiers were told to do whatever would best destroy the will of the people to resist, and would cost the least money. The thing they hit on was raping the women. They raped at least two hundred thousand Bengali women, and they did it purposefully, as a matter of military strategy. These were rapes planned in advance and efficiently carried out under orders. A report by Joyce Goldman in *The New York Times Magazine* (July 23, 1972) stated that the troops were often shown pornographic films before being turned loose on women rounded up in buildings, in order to stimulate them enough to carry out their orders to rape.

After the war, of course, their husbands and families did not take back the raped women—now named National Heroines. They are living in camps or with kind people in the urban areas. The rapes that caused them to be called heroines also caused them to be disgraced in the eyes of their people. Some of those who became pregnant were given abortions, but since the first groups that offered refuge to these women were Roman Catholic missions, large numbers of them were not given abortions, but have borne the children of rape.

A variation of this sort of rape is rumored to exist in this country. We have been informed that organized crime uses rape or the threat of rape to terrorize people and extort payments. If you do not pay, you, or your wife or daughter or sister, will be raped. It is a fairly safe method, since the rapists are almost never taken to court and, once there, are almost never convicted.

There are also what might be called political rapes. Eldridge Cleaver, in *Soul on Ice,* explained that he raped white women in order to attack the white man.

> I became a rapist. To refine my technique and modus operandi, I started out by practicing on black girls in the ghetto . . . and when I considered myself smooth enough, I crossed the tracks and sought out white prey. I did this consciously, deliberately, willfully, methodically—though looking back I see that I was in a frantic, wild, and completely abandoned frame of mind.
>
> Rape was an insurrectionary act. It delighted me that I was defying and trampling upon the white man's law, upon his system of values, and that I was defiling his women—and this point, I believe, was the most satisfying to me because I was very resentful over the historical fact of how the white man has used the black woman. I felt I was getting revenge.

Here, the victim of the rape was no more than a means through which the black man attacked the white man. If any more evidence is required to show that women do not really exist as human beings for some men, there is Cleaver's admission that he raped black women for practice. Where was his black consciousness when he raped black sisters for practice? It was there, but it was a *man's* black consciousness. Women, of any color, are objects to be used in the war between man and man.

It would be difficult to argue that either the West Pakistani soldiers or Eldridge Cleaver was sexually disturbed. They were simply men damaging other men's property. If they had felt that they could achieve the same purpose in some other way, by destroying other objects, they would probably have done so.

In all these cases, sex is at best a secondary motivation for rape. The primary reason for each of these men attacking a woman had nothing to do with her as an individual. These women were raped because they were Bengali women, enemy women, white women. They were objects in a male power struggle.

There is yet another kind of rape in which other men and the effect of rape on them are more important than the woman who happens to be the victim. This is the sort of ritual rape that goes by the name "gang rape" in America, "pack rape" in Australia, and other names in other places. In these rapes a victim is chosen at random by a group of men or boys who need or want to prove something to each other.

A case which came to our attention while we were writing this book shows very clearly how this kind of rape works. We have tried as much as possible to avoid telling gruesome stories: we do not feel that it is necessary for us to go into the horrors of rape. That is done often enough in the newspapers, and besides, most women know all too well what those horrors are. But in this case, to tell the story is to tell the horrors.

In a university town in the Midwest there is a training center which deals with, among others, the mentally retarded. One of the students at that center was a young woman of twenty-five with a mental age of eleven years. She was from a farm in the outlying area, but she lived in an apartment by herself in town. She had few friends, which is true of many people afflicted with mental retardation. At some time, however, she met a couple of men from a fraternity house on the campus who struck up an acquaintance with her. This acquaintance ended, we were told, in her being taken to the fraternity house and used sexually by about forty men, members of that fraternity and others. The "men" also attempted to force intercourse between her and a dog, and they put bottles and other objects up her vagina. For reasons best known to themselves, they then took her to a police station and charged her with prostitution, offering to drop the charges if she were institutionalized. She was.

The story first came to light when one of the fraternity members bragged about it to another man in one of his classes. He misjudged the other man, who was horrified and told the story to one of the professors. A group was formed to confront the fraternity with the charge. At first, the fraternity men admitted that it had all happened, but they protested that she had done it of her own free will. A woman with a mental age of eleven, alone and with a need for friendship and affection that was not being filled, gave her consent to the things we described above, they said, and so the thirty or forty adult college men who did them were innocent. Later, when the whole thing was made public, they denied the story altogether. The woman, meanwhile, was in an institution where, upon discovering that she was pregnant, she had a complete emotional breakdown.

Protest against the fraternity was taken up by a women's group on campus, but neither the police nor the university would take any action against any of the individuals or the fraternity. It was requested that the fraternity be thrown off campus as a gesture indicating that the university did not condone their actions. This was not done. One cannot help but wonder what the university would have done if the same group had been accused of open homosexual activity.

We have told this story in order to show what normal, red-blooded American boys are capable of doing, not in isolation, not in dark and lonely alleys, not in the jungles of Vietnam, but in their own fraternity house with the approval and participation of their peers. These were not men who had no other access to sexual activity (a letter from one of their girl friends, defending them, was published in the school newspaper). They were not deviants in any usual meaning of that term. They are graduating from that university and going out to assume their places in the young executive club, in the research laboratory, and in the political arena.

This was a group activity. Who can doubt that these same young men would, almost to a man, have had considerable qualms about doing these things to the woman by themselves? They would probably have felt that what they were doing was perverse and shameful. It was the presence of the other men that made the act acceptable; in fact, it was probably only the presence of the other men that made it attractive. Each one of them would, undoubtedly, have preferred to go to bed with a woman to whom they were more attracted than this mentally retarded woman. Only when they were together, with their friends, was the idea appealing. And it was the sort of appeal that baiting a dog, or watching a hanging, holds.

Another widespread practice was reported in Susan Griffin's article. This is the ritual rape at a stag party given for a man who is about to be married. It is not uncommon, at such parties, for a dancer to be hired for entertainment, and then for the bridegroom to be expected to rape her. The report from a woman who was involved in one of these events indicated that the bridegroom himself did not seem to be at all eager to do it, but, though she fought, begged, and claimed to have a venereal disease, he grimly went ahead. He had to save face in front of the other men.

We will not tell any more of the dozens of similar stories that we came across in researching the book. It is enough to say, simply, that rape is often part of a male ritual, like initiation, or chugging beer. Amir reported this phenomenon in his book. In Amir's study, 25 percent of the rapes were group rapes, and 97.1 percent of them were planned. They follow a definite pattern in which one man, usually the acknowledged leader of the group, seems to sanction the behavior of the others. Group rapes are usually characterized by considerable brutality, even though this is the one situation in which no brutality, no threat even, would be necessary to subdue the victim. The brutality seems part of the dehumanization of the victim. And it is most necessary in this sort of rape to make sure that none of the other men sees the victim as anything more than a contemptible object.

It is time, then, for women to stop thinking of rapists as sick or crazy men. You might very easily have dated one of the men in that fraternity, or your daughter might, or your older sister. That bridegroom might have been the man that you married, or the men who egged him on might have been friends of yours. The rapist *is* the man next door.

He in a few minutes ravished this fair creature, or at least would have ravished her, if she had not, by a timely compliance, prevented him.
Henry Fielding

A little still she strove, and much repented,
And whispering "I will ne'er consent"—consented.
Lord Byron, *Don Juan*

CHAPTER FOUR

Rape and Social Patterns

The woman was eighteen years old, a college freshman, and a virgin. She had been rather strictly brought up, but she was strong-willed and was testing her freedom. That night she went to a fraternity party with a young man she had dated a few times before. He told her it would be a long party, lasting beyond the dormitory closing hours, and so he had arranged for her to spend the night with the girl friend of one of his fraternity brothers. After some hesitation, she signed out overnight. It was the first time she had ever done that, and it seemed exciting.

The party did end very late. When it was over, her date informed her that his fraternity brother was going to spend the night with his girl friend, so she couldn't go there. The dormitory had already been closed for hours.

He offered to rent her a room in a motel. Knowing that he would meet with some resistance, he talked to her for a long time, reassuring her that it would be all right and that he had no intention of coming in with her. She couldn't go back to the dormitory without waking her dorm mother and risking getting campused. Her date really managed to make it seem that she would be making a fuss over nothing if she did not accept his offer. Of course he played on her fears of seeming unsophisticated and naïve. And so, not knowing how to say that she didn't trust him without offending him, she said that she would do it. It was really too bad, she thought, that she couldn't rent the room herself and just leave him in the parking lot. But she never had much money and she certainly didn't carry the price of a motel room in her purse when she was going to a party. Besides, she didn't even know how you went about renting motel rooms, or whether they would rent one to an eighteen-year-old girl.

When they got to the motel, he walked her to her room. She was a little afraid of the strange motel, so that was all right with her. But when they got to the room, he didn't leave; he walked in and closed the door behind him. She asked him to leave, of course. He said that he just wanted to sit down for a minute before he drove back to the fraternity house. He had paid for the room, after all, and it wasn't very generous of her to ask him to get out when all he wanted to do was sit down for a minute.

They talked for a little while. He was very natural, casual, and relaxed. He didn't try to do anything, but she was still uneasy. Finally he got up to leave. He came over to kiss her good night. Well, she thought, she had kissed him before when they had gone out. So she kissed him, trying to be firm but friendly. That was when he pushed her onto the bed, pulled up her skirt, pinned her down, and raped her.

She fought. In fact, she fought very hard, but she was already on her back and it didn't do much good. He was quite a bit bigger and stronger than she was. At that point she really didn't have a chance.

It hurt a lot. He told her to stop moving. She said she couldn't stop, it hurt too much. She wasn't moving on purpose. By that time she had given up the idea of fighting him off. At no time did he seem to be overcome by desire. He didn't say anything nice to her, but he didn't say anything bad either. Only that she should stop moving. He was annoyed that she wouldn't lie still.

At any time during the attack she might have grabbed the lamp from the bedside table and hit him over the head. She didn't. When it was over, he rolled over and went to sleep. She lay on the bed beside him, not moving, not sleeping, until morning.

Do you believe that the woman in this story wanted to be raped? The man who raped her did. In fact, he did not believe that he had raped her. If you agree with him, if you think she got what she wanted, maybe you can suggest when she should have started fighting. When he said he would walk her to her room? When he came into the room and said he wanted to sit down for a while before he went back? When he kissed her good night? The first two are too soon. There just wasn't any threat of rape. She would have had no reason to start fighting him off when he was doing nothing directly threatening to her. She might have refused to kiss him good night, but that would only have brought on the problem earlier. It wouldn't have solved anything. By the time he had pushed her onto the bed, it was too late.

Or perhaps you think she should have picked up the lamp from the bedside table and hit him over the head. Do you think it would have stunned him? That would have been ideal. Perhaps it would have shown him that she meant what she said and that she was not to be pushed around. Or maybe it would just have made him angry, angry enough to beat her up. On the other hand, it might have killed him. Then what would she do? Call the police and say, "I was in this motel room with this guy and he tried to rape me so I killed him"?

This woman was really in a trap, and she was supposed to be. Once in, she behaved pretty much as she had to behave. Her mistakes were earlier mistakes.

First, she should not have been involved in the existing dating situation, which is set up so that the man controls everything. Only years of accepting that kind of situation could have made this woman allow the man to determine where she would spend the night in the first place. No sensible woman, if she ever thought about it, would allow the roof over her head to be dependent on a man with whom she has had only a short acquaintance, a man she has no reason to trust. And no adult should *need* someone else to arrange where she is going to lay her head. But in the present dating system women commonly expect men to take care of them, and therefore situations develop in which a woman can't take care of herself. This leaves her vulnerable to men she may scarcely know.

She should also have provided herself with the money for a motel room. A young man who was as short of funds as the woman in our story wouldn't have gone out that night. If he did, he would at least have been able to take care of himself. When a woman is financially dependent on a man, even if it is only for one evening, she puts herself, to some extent, in his power. (Then too, of course, a young man would not have been in quite the same predicament anyway. They don't lock young college men out of their dormitories.)

Assume that she did not make the first two mistakes and that she had no other place to stay. Then she should have gone back to the dormitory and roused her dorm mother. Her main reason for not doing so was the desire not to give anyone trouble. She didn't want to inconvenience anyone. This woman put herself into a situation where, if she had allowed herself to think about it, she would have known that she could get into terrible trouble, just to avoid waking someone up for ten minutes to open the door for her. Consideration for others is a nice thing, but in women it sometimes takes on utterly nonsensical proportions.

This woman may have been incredibly naïve, and she may have been gullible, but she was trapped before she walked into that motel room. She was trapped before she accepted her first date with this man. She was trapped by the way she thought about herself and the way she thought about men, by a ritual of courtship that she had been taught when she reached puberty, or before. And she was trapped by the way the man started thinking about women when he was about five. She was trapped, and she was most definitely raped.

It is this kind of rape that causes the most confusion. It and the other cases like it form the fuzzy border line separating heterosexual intercourse as we know it from rape. This woman's case is clearer than many. We realize that, to insure that this book is taken seriously by those people who will be very ready to criticize us, it would probably be better to ignore this sort of rape altogether. However, we believe that this is rape, and that it is so familiar an experience to most women that we have an obligation to talk about it. It also helps to make clear just why so much confusion exists when people try to distinguish rape from the rest of the sexual relations between men and women.

In the time-honored pattern, men and women in our society go out into the world seeking Love. Both soon find that it is not immediately apparent just what Love is, or how and where it is to be found. So, after a while, the search for Love is set aside in favor of more tangible things. The system we are about to describe may have been recently updated, but for a surprising number of people it remains accurate even today.

The woman wanted some sort of security: a man, a steady, a husband. In order to obtain these, she bartered with her body. She made herself attractive so that some male would become interested in her. At first, the rules specified that he might look but not touch. The barter advanced from there. If a male offered a date, she allowed a certain amount of sexual gratification, but not too much. As he offered more security, getting pinned, becoming engaged, she reciprocated by allowing him to "go further." But not until he actually married her, and she had him signed, sealed, and delivered, did she relinquish her virginity. Thereafter, she bartered sex, the comforts of home, and whatever status she could contribute in exchange for food, shelter, and protection for herself and her children. That, put very bluntly, used to be the woman's role in courtship and marriage patterns.

The male, on the other hand, when he isn't seeking Love, is seeking sex. And that means sex under whatever conditions the particular man can stand. Whether in a whorehouse or the back seat of a Toyota, the object is to score. However, your score counts more if you don't pay for it in cold hard cash. The most respected player in the game is the one who best outwits the most females by coaxing, lying, maneuvering; the one who, with the least actual cost to himself, gets the most females to give him the most sex.

The woman is solely and completely responsible for stopping him. She is also responsible if he presumes that she isn't really trying to stop him and therefore forces her. The woman is placed in an impossible situation. She is responsible for her actions, his actions, his interpretations of her actions—in short, for everything that could possibly give him an excuse to "lose control."

This situation has been accepted for a long time. Men, it is said, just *are* that way. They can't control themselves. Any man who can must be just a little strange. That is why, in the days before the sexual revolution, when a girl was necking, there were certain limits that she had to enforce. Opinions varied from one social group to another as to just what a boy could stand before he lost control. In one group it was his hand on her breast, under her blouse, but not under her bra.

That was very conservative. In another, he could maintain control of himself if he touched a girl above the waist only, provided he used just his hands. Another group declared that *anything* above the waist was all right. Young boys had a remarkable variation in breaking points, depending on the conventions of their particular group.

The "sexual revolution" affected these patterns in some ways, but not always for the better. Sex is not necessarily a thing that women use only to barter for security, although now they often use it to barter for Love. Women have supposedly been freed, freed to enjoy sex, to operate sexually as independent human beings. But sexual freedom does not exist in a vacuum. The woman who has been given sexual freedom without real financial and social independence will find herself still bartering. The woman who has attained sexual independence but has not yet freed herself from the destructive elements involved in her emotional relations to men will find herself still tied to old ways of relating sexually.

Women are not yet fully independent people. At times they are just independent enough to get themselves into dangerous predicaments. The young woman in our story had that sort of independence. Her mother would not have been free to make the kind of decisions that led her to that motel room. But a really independent woman would have had the option of avoiding the situation if she found it threatening. Many young girls declare their independence by leaving home, but they are not independent enough to survive on their own and their sisters are not organized enough to take care of them. Out of necessity, these girls depend on men they don't trust in situations they know are dangerous. And often they get raped. In coming out of their previously sheltered existence, they are suddenly faced with problems they don't know how to handle.

One reason for the startling increase in rape cases in the past ten years is this meeting of the old sexual mores and the new. In the old order, certain women were respectable and all others were fair game. When they reject the standards of respectability, when they don't wear bras, when they go to bars by themselves, when they walk down the street after a certain hour, they are marked for fair game. Too many women just don't realize this. That is the reason for the outrageously high record of rapes among female hitchhikers. For the men who pick up hitchhikers and follow through, this kind of sexual encounter is not rape. Rape does not apply to a woman who falls outside the limits of respectability; she is just a free lay.

The protections that were built into the old society have been discarded as restrictive, but they have not been replaced. The man who was a seducer was once maligned as much as the rapist, but not any longer. That idea was discarded along with the one that women are innocent creatures who must be protected against designing males. The world has now given women credit for deciding for themselves when they want to have sex with a man, credit for the intelligence to judge for themselves what a man's intentions are. But what has really happened is that *all* responsibility has been taken away from the man.

Deception, which was once considered as evil as rape, is now just one more weapon in a man's arsenal. If a woman is deceived, it is her own fault. She is still not allowed really to say yes; she is expected to require some seduction, and so she is not believed when she says no. A woman can say no all day, but if she has gotten herself into what, by Victorian standards, is a compromising situation, she will not be believed. At the present time, the rapist has the best of both worlds— women who are taking more risks, and a society which says that if they take those risks they deserve whatever they get.

It is not enough just to loosen things up a bit sexually. As long as man is the hunter and woman is the game, doing away with restrictions on women only makes it more likely that women will be raped, not less. As long as the male is sexually predatory, no woman is safe from the kind of rape encountered by the woman in our story. In fact, every act of sexual intercourse with that sort of man is a kind of rape. We talked to wives who felt that they had never made love with their husbands but had only been raped.

We would prefer to suggest that men are not beasts, that they are quite capable of controlling themselves, and that it is not the woman's responsibility to do it for them. We would prefer to establish that, if women flirt, they are not inviting rape. If they kiss a man good night, they are not inviting rape. Even, and this should raise a few male hackles, even if they should be guilty of "teasing" a man, they are not inviting rape. Men know that, even if women don't. They know that they don't "get out of control." That myth has provided a convenient way for them to evade responsibility for their own sexual actions.

Hey, baby, where ya goin', whatcha doin', what's hap-
penin'? Ya lookin' good, sugar. Nice ass. Looka them
legs. Wanna give me some? Mama. Hey, look at those.
Where's your bra, honey? Don't they get cold that way?
I'll keep 'em warm. What have you got there? What a
nice piece. Wanna drink? Where ya goin' so fast? Can I
come too? Ha, ha, ha. Ain't ya goin' ta talk to us? Ain't
ya even gonna smile? Whatsa matter with you? You
stuck up, or something? Think you're too good, huh?
Ugly bitch anyway, fat legs . . . Hey, wanna come up
ta my house? Show ya a really good time. You got real
nice legs, honey. Got anything between 'em for me? . . .
Hey, look at that one. What a pig . . . Hey, you. Your
blouse is undone. Whoooeeee. Ain't ya gonna give me a
peek? Bouncy, bouncy, bouncy. Doin' anythin' tonight?
How much? Huh? How much for it? Ten bucks? Five?
Hey, whatsa matter with you? I'm just trying to be
friendly.

Really, you know, most women sort of like that kind of
thing. It's a compliment. Like all the women I know who
go to Italy and come back talking about all the men who
pinched them on the ass. They like it . . .
    A Chicago talk-show commentator

CHAPTER FIVE

The Little Rapes

You are walking down a city street, your own street, not far from home. As you turn the corner, you look up the street quickly, studying it, and then you look back down at the sidewalk. You walk a few steps, thinking and planning, and then you glance up to check out the first obstacle—three men standing on the sidewalk a few doors up. Will they step aside to let you pass? Are they going to make some comment? One of them catches your eye. You look back at the sidewalk, pretending that you weren't watching him. It's always bad if someone catches you looking at him. Maybe you should cross the street. A glance over there tells you that you can't do that either. There's a group of teenagers hanging around in front of one of the houses. You had better take your chances with the three men.

You are still looking down at the sidewalk, but you can feel that one man staring at you. You know his friends have stopped talking and are beginning to notice you. You wonder if they will start making comments among themselves. You don't want to have to go past them, but on the other hand you don't want to walk past the bunch of teenagers either. It would be too humiliatingly obvious for you to turn around at this point and go back. So you take a deep breath and move over to the edge of the sidewalk, hoping they'll let you go by.

"Hey, honey, where ya goin'? Can I go too?"

"Ain't ya cold, with that short skirt and all?"

49

"C'mon and talk to us awhile. We ain't gonna hurt ya. You're not very friendly."

You keep your head down and pretend not to hear them, while your face burns with embarrassment. Your body tenses as you wait for a hand to reach out, but you make it past them physically untouched. You start fumbling in your purse, pretending that you are looking for something; what you are really doing is waiting to hear a footstep behind you. There is nothing. They're not going to come after you. You've made it.

There's only a little way to go before you get home, and no one else is on the side of the street between you and your front door. Of course, there's still that group of kids across the street, but they don't look like a gang. As a matter of fact, they don't look energetic enough to cross the street. They'll probably just say something, but you'll be far enough away to make a good show of ignoring them. Despite that, you feel some apprehension.

Not a sound. No hoots, no whistles. There's a chance you won't even be noticed.

"Wow. Hey, look! Hey, you, whatcha doin'?"

Are they crossing over? No. It's all right then. You're almost home. You're on your front step, your key in your hand. You walk into your apartment, flop down on the couch, and relax. You've made it home again without anyone giving you a really hard time.

Rape, as we have defined it, is any sexual intimacy, whether by direct physical contact or not, that is forced on one person by another. If you are subjected (many of us are) to this kind of violation every day, a gradual erosion begins—an erosion of your self-respect and privacy. You lose a little when you are shaken out of your daydreams by the whistles and comments of the construction workers you have to pass. You lose a little when a junior executive looks down your blouse or gives you a familiar pat at work. You lose a little to the obnoxious drunk at the next table, to that man on the subway, to the guys in the drive-in.

In themselves these incidents are disgusting, repellent—in fact, intolerable. Acceptance of them as normal is dangerous. This is one of the many ways in which women are *prepared* to be victims.

Learning to avoid being hassled in the street is as much a part of living in the city as learning to cope with public transportation. To see a black man in the South (or in the North) subjected to this kind of abuse would make one sick. It would be painful to watch him as he lowers his head and tries to get past a group of whites unmolested. Today blacks are no longer expected to "know their place," although deliberate humiliation and discrimination against them still exists. But women face this same kind of badgering and taunting, and accept it. They have come to think of it as an unavoidable part of life.

The reasons for this are complex. They certainly include the fear of actual physical attack, but they also derive from something much more subtle. Early in our lives there is instilled in us a desire to please, or at least a desire not to offend. This is not part of our nature; it is drilled into us from the moment we are dressed in pink booties. And it is done well. We reach maturity with a sometimes-pathetic desire to please others. Even when we have otherwise overcome our rigid stereotyping, we have this need for approval. It can be debilitating, and can twist our lives in undreamed-of ways.

And so we think we have to be pleasant to the man in the street who approaches us. We have been taught not to displease anyone. Later, when we try to explain how we got ourselves into such situations, we usually mention that we were afraid of physical attack. That is something that others will understand, but it is not always the reason behind our actions. We often back down and capitulate when the threat of attack is minimal.

Consider the subway-car or bus-riding molester. These men are so maddeningly present in any major urban center that many women have run into several. Every woman can tell a story about the man who sat beside her with a newspaper shielding his open fly, or can talk about those mysterious hands that suddenly appear from under attaché cases, coats, or simply out of nowhere. The astonishing thing is not that there are so many men who have the nerve or the inclination to do this, but that women are so often intimidated by these disembodied hands and fake sleepers.

Part of the problem is that women are afraid of drawing attention to themselves. How often have they endured these men rather than make a scene? If the woman does make a scene, the man should be humiliated by having attention drawn to what he is doing, but somehow he never is. He will calmly close his coat and join the other passengers in staring at an obviously crazy woman. *She* is the one who feels degraded. And it seems that she can bear a lot of degradation as long as she is the only one who knows about it.

This kind of man rarely threatens any further attack. Crowded subways and buses are not the ideal places for a man to attack or rape a woman. But even without fear of physical harm, women put up with the maulings. They have been conditioned to be afraid of men under any circumstances and to be afraid of offending them even when there is no possible basis for their fear.

One woman told us that she allowed herself to be taken into a dark alley because she was afraid of offending the man by implying that he might rape her. He did. In retrospect the woman seems terribly naïve. But put yourself in her place at that moment and remember all of the similar situations in which you did not "rudely" avoid a man for fear of offending him. It is this kind of everyday occurrence that sets women up to be raped.

What happens if you are walking down the street and a strange man tries to pick you up? However charming and friendly he may be, there is always the potential for hostility on his part if he meets with a strongly negative reaction from you. As long as you are polite and play the game, his aggression will not appear; but if you tell the man to leave you alone—as you have every right to do—be prepared for the unexpected. He thinks that your role requires you to play along. He wants to think that he will actually get your phone number, at least your name, perhaps even a date. It is a difficult game for a woman to play, requiring ingenuity, energy, and charm. Most likely you feel obliged to play it with any man who wants to take up your time.

Perhaps he will open with "Mind if I walk with you?" It is a perfectly polite question, but you don't want to get to know this man, and besides, you make it a rule not to speak to strangers in the street. So you try to get rid of him. You say something on the order of "You seem like a nice fellow and all, but I would rather be alone." Remember, it is *his* behavior that is unacceptable. He wouldn't dare to start a conversation like this with another *man,* and you wouldn't go up to a stranger either. It should be assumed that someone walking along the street is going somewhere and not out looking for conversation. Yet this stranger has felt free to approach you and try to talk to you. You have so far responded with a politely discouraging answer.

He returns with "I just wanted to talk to you." How do you counter that? You could simply tell him the truth. "I don't think you understood me before. I'm not interested in talking to you." But that would sound rude. (Isn't it remarkable that when you insist on controlling your own time, you are being rude, but when a man insists on taking up your time, he is being friendly?) Instead you will probably smile and say something a little less determined. "Honestly, I have some things I want to think about." He neatly returns, "Why don't you tell me about them? Maybe I can help."

This will go on as long as you keep it up, or as long as he remains interested. By the time you get rid of him (*if* you get rid of him), your walk will have been spoiled and you will be frustrated and annoyed. Worse, once you are trapped into his game, you can find yourself in a dangerous situation. If you were so afraid of offending the man that you allowed him to waste your time, what are you going to do when he suggests going into that alley? Perhaps that is an exaggerated case, but often the confrontation ends in his trying to get you to invite him into your apartment or to go to his. If you are still playing on the level of "No, really, I just don't want to go to your place. I have other things to do," instead of saying, "Get lost!" you are in serious trouble.

If there is any doubt remaining about the underlying quality of the game, consider what would happen if you didn't know how to play and you responded with civilized propriety. The man makes small talk, and you presume that he is simply friendly and sociable. He asks you, "What are you doing tonight?" You make the appropriate answer and politely return the question. "I'm probably going to watch TV. What are you going to do?" Now this man will inevitably assume, on the basis of that response, that you want to go out with him, and probably even go to bed with him. You can tell him you are perfectly happy watching television by yourself. You can tell him you don't know him well enough to have him over. You can tell him you're planning to go to Mars as soon as All in the Family is over. He won't hear you. You made a wrong move in the game, and you will never get rid of him.

The only way to avoid all of this is to demand from the very beginning the right to your own time, to your own life. Don't get into the game at all. It is really nothing more than a matter of simple self-respect. If you really believe in your own worth as a human being, the problem will take care of itself.

It is difficult, however, to achieve that self-respect. It is not a part of the feminine ideal. A woman who believes that she belongs to herself will be described as cold, hard, unfeeling, stuck-up, bitchy, or, worst of all, aggressive. Women are not supposed to take care of themselves, to be independent. They are taught that it is appealing to be weak, that it is attractive to be helpless. Few people would object to a little boy's learning to defend himself, but in a group of women who had gathered together to work against rape, one woman worried about encouraging women to learn self-defense because, she said, it would be a "brutalizing" experience. Most women have encountered that attitude before and have been affected by it.

And no wonder. Women are inundated from all sides with the glorification of female vulnerability. Not long ago there was a fashion spread in one of the young women's magazines which featured the "vulnerable" look. The clothing was all very soft, very clinging, and very small. The models huddled in corners, shrank against looming walls.

Until recently most women wore high heels that made it difficult for them to move and skirts that made it impossible for them to walk naturally. They wore, and still wear, undergarments that make it hard for them to breathe and even harder for them to digest their food. Their legs freeze in the winter; they stifle in girdles in the summer. Not only do they do all of this for the sake of beauty, but the very idea of beauty that our society (and its media) offers upholds suffering as appealingly feminine.

Are we saying that women must give up being attractive? Absolutely not. But think about it. Who do women want to be attractive to, and in what way? There was once an image of the attractive American woman that was different from the one that now exists. She was strong. She was independent. She was capable. And the way she looked reflected the way she was. The models were Katharine Hepburn, Greta Garbo, Rosalind Russell, Joan Crawford. They were women who actually walked when they wanted to move from one place to another. They worked beside men and they played beside them. They shook hands when they met a man, instead of simpering at him. They were strong and beautiful. No one ever dreamed of putting Katharine Hepburn or Greta Garbo in a movie where she would be drugged, put into a cowpen, and sold like a side of beef.

It is time for women to take their lives into their own hands and start fighting for their self-respect, not only because that is the best way for any human being to live, but also because to live any other way is damned dangerous. Women accept too many things as simply "the way things are." The condition of their lives has become intolerable. All the daily encroachments on their existence as human beings, whether subtle or blatant, prepare them to be victims of rape. Even men on the street expect them to be soothers and ego-inflaters and fantasy objects. If they refuse, they're man-haters. But what if they play the game, placate every stranger, and learn to accept the role? What if they become what men want them to be? With that image of themselves, how are women to act when the game gets pushed a little further, and further still: when it becomes rape? The confusion sets in then. Should I struggle? Why should I fight? What am I fighting for? What am I fighting for that I haven't given up already?

The time for a woman to start fighting is before she gives it all up— fighting for the right to herself, her pride, her body, her time.

When I asked Berkeley, California's Police Inspector in charge of rape investigation if he knew why men rape women, he replied that he had not spoken with "these people and delved into what really makes them tick, because that really isn't my job . . ." However, when I asked him how a woman might prevent being raped, he was not so reticent. "I wouldn't advise any woman to go walking around alone at night . . . and she should lock her car at all times." The Inspector illustrated his warning with a grisly story about a man who lay in wait for women in the back seats of their cars, while they were shopping in the local supermarket. This man eventually murdered one of his rape victims. "Always lock your car," the Inspector repeated, and then added, without a hint of irony, "Of course, you don't have to get paranoid about this type of thing."

Susan Griffin, "Rape: The All-American Crime"

CHAPTER SIX

Precautions and Preventions

"Once in a Cabinet," Israeli Prime Minister Golda Meir related, "we had to deal with the fact that there had been an outbreak of assaults on women at night. One minister . . . suggested a curfew; women should stay at home after dark. I said, 'But it's the men who are attacking the women. If there's to be a curfew let the men stay at home, not the women.' "

As Prime Minister Meir pointed out, in talking about preventing rape, it is an absurdity to talk about restricting women. However, since it is unlikely that there will be any restriction on men in the near future, and since women should not have to adapt to the present intolerable situation, it is necessary to discuss what women themselves can do to reduce the possibility of being raped.

Most women are familiar with calculated risks; birth control is one of the most obvious examples. If you don't want to get pregnant, there are a number of things you can do. The only foolproof method is not to have heterosexual intercourse. The pill is very effective, but it has some definite disadvantages, as does the IUD. The diaphragm and foam are not so effective, but they are safer for your body and better than nothing at all. The rhythm method may also be better than nothing, but that is debatable.

As for preventing rape, there are a number of options there too. You could lead a hermit's existence or live in a cloister. Then the chances are fairly good that you won't be raped. Like the pill, this way is not 100 percent effective, but it is as close as you are likely to get. If that, or any close approximation of that, is the way you want to live, you may as well stop reading now.

There is a second option. You might take a very good self-defense course and work at becoming strong, healthy, and skilled in karate and street fighting. You'd have more confidence and be able to think more clearly in any situation. You would still have to be careful, but your life wouldn't be as restricted as it is now. You may still run into an impossible situation; if you are confronted with a gang of armed men, you lose. But in most circumstances it will give you the necessary edge to properly defend yourself.

Finally, you can try to understand what rape is. You can learn how and when it is likely to happen, and how your manner of relating to men can lead you into the kind of situation in which rape occurs. We hope that some of what we have said in the first chapters of this book will help you to do that. At the same time, you can begin to take some of the common-sense precautions we will discuss in this chapter. You can also learn some elementary self-defense. Equally important, you can learn what to do if you or one of your friends is raped, so that a frightening, dehumanizing event is not made worse by those who try to "help" afterward.

Let's begin with simple, straightforward suggestions for better self-protection without serious restrictions. If you are to be secure, it should surely be in your home. Unfortunately, this is where rapes commonly take place. Sometimes the intruder comes in with the intention of raping. Sometimes the rape is an afterthought, with burglary as the primary motive for the break-in. With some care, the chances of such an occurrence can be minimized.

The most basic and important rule is to have strong locks on all accessible doors and windows, and to use them. Still, an ordinary window lock won't secure a window that is loose in its frame. In that case, install a deadbolt lock on the side of the frame. Many people are careless about locks. Because they are restricted in so many ways, they sometimes rebel at trivial things. Locking doors and windows is not a guarantee that no one will ever break into a house, but the prowler who has neither extraordinary dexterity nor unlimited time will find it too difficult. There are always enough people who do leave their doors unlocked.

Another good idea is to have a peephole installed in the door, and to accustom yourself to using it. If you don't automatically check the peephole before opening the door, you're neglecting one of the best forms of protection. A safety chain is not as good as a peephole, but it is better than nothing. Many safety chains give the illusion of security, but can be snapped or ripped out of the doorframe with a solid shove. So be certain that you have a heavy one and that it is properly installed, with *long* screws. We stress the idea of a peephole because it is more realistic to prepare to keep out an intruder yourself than to construct an elaborate burglar-alarm system. The Boston Strangler simply checked through apartment houses looking for women's names on the mailboxes, rang the bell, and posed as a serviceman or deliveryman. He claimed to have found over three hundred victims in this or a similar manner. Don't put your first name on your mailbox or in the telephone directory; and, before allowing a serviceman into your home, ask for his identification. If for some reason he doesn't carry identification, call his office (most workers who ask to gain access to the homes of strangers will carry identification). There is no reason to feel foolish about this procedure. Any legitimate repairman has encountered hundreds of women who were wary of letting strangers into their homes. You are not the first to question him, and even if you were the first, your objection would be valid.

The simplest and most direct way for a man to gain entry into your house is to find where you have hidden the spare key. If you must have a spare key concealed outside, at least use some imagination in choosing a place to hide it. Don't leave it in a flowerpot, under a doormat, in the mailbox, or over the doorjamb.

Another often-neglected matter of common sense is keeping the shades drawn—perhaps because our mothers said it to us so often that we think of it as a puritan hang-up. A peeping tom is disconcerting, but a more real problem is the fact that you are advertising that you are alone in your apartment.

Outside your home, things become more complicated. In dealing with the men who say crude things or try to pick you up, it is best to respond with all the annoyance, boredom, and contempt you can muster. The most devastating thing you can do to a macho is to make him feel stupid. For example, if the person bothering you is particularly young, you could look him straight in the eye and demand, "How old *are* you?" Don't be thrown off by any line he may come up with; don't let him impress you. If he dodges, repeat, "How *old* are you?" If you're confronted with an ordinary middle-aged man, call him a fat creep, not a male chauvinist pig. The latter he may delight in, the former will make him feel like a fat creep. Don't show that you are upset or embarrassed. That is part of what he is looking for. What he is not looking for is contempt. Perhaps it is best to react the way you did when you last stepped into dog shit on the sidewalk.

If you're walking down a dark street, it is best to walk near the curb, away from alleys, not so much to avoid being grabbed from an alley, but to avoid being pushed into one. If you are passing a possible source of danger, look at it. The same goes if you think you are being followed. If there is actually any danger, you will be able to see it and prepare to deal with it. A block or two of thinking that someone is following you will get you so rattled that you won't be able to do anything if it is true. If there isn't any danger, of course, you can relax. The normal reaction to a threatening situation is to hunch your shoulders, put your head down, and try not to look frightened. Don't look frightened—look alert. Don't do foolishly careless things just so you won't look paranoid. If there is actually someone watching you, you have reason to be taking precautions. And he knows it.

Beware of strange men out to protect you. This includes the man who accosts you on a dark street and tells you grisly tales of women just like you who were walking through this very neighborhood at this very time of night. After he has you upset and muddled, he will undoubtedly offer to walk or drive you home. The same game can be played by men who work in pairs. In Boston, on the trains, a pair operated this way: one man would make obvious leers and gestures at a woman passenger. The other man would tell the woman that she should "look out for" the first man; he would offer to get off the train with her if she was followed. She was, and the two men then took turns. This particular pair was integrated. You can guess who played which role.

If, for any reason, you decide to accept a man's offer of help, let him walk you home, not drive you. And don't let him go all the way to your front door. While walking with him, look at him, and keep out of his reach. If he is gallantly walking on the outside of the sidewalk and you have to pass an alley, either step to the outside yourself or drop a step behind him. Don't ever let him drop behind you. It is a good idea not to let him walk on the outside anyway. That was a nice gesture in the Middle Ages when people threw their garbage out of the window and the one on the outside was likely to be hit by it. But when you are with a strange man, you want your avenue of escape unblocked.

A similar situation arises when you turn to a man for help in arranging something outside normal channels. You might be a runaway, or you might be trying to arrange an abortion. Not only are you frightened and dependent on the man, but you are usually in no position to report him to the police or to make your situation known. If you need an abortion, contact a women's group. If you are a runaway, and you can't find any women to help you, be very careful about the men who offer to. If you possibly can, get hold of some money before you leave home. No one is as vulnerable as an underage woman without any means of support. There is no sense in trusting a strange man simply because he doesn't look like a rapist. What does a rapist look like?

If you are molested or otherwise hassled by a man who is connected with a group that is organized to help people, you should report him to that group. Perhaps nothing will happen to him, but since you may not be able to report him to the police, exposing him is about the best you can do. Maybe that group will think twice about putting other young girls at his disposal.

Every urban woman is wary of public transportation. The subway molesters prey on her tolerance, and they are usually met with mortified silence. They particularly choose young girls or women who seem timid. Once these men meet with solid opposition, they almost invariably back down; there is no reason to tolerate them.

At your next encounter, don't pretend his hand is only accidentally touching you. Don't make a subtle shift and retreat against the wall. Don't take his hand off your leg only to have him touch you again. No. Stand up and yell, "YOU GODDAMN PERVERT, YOU'RE DISGUST-ING!" Won't that be exhilarating? The man will go through the hell of discovery, and maybe he won't sidle up to another victim the next time he gets on the subway.

If you've ever watched people on buses, you will have noticed some definite patterns in the way people choose seats. Barring any dramatic outside influences (blinding light, drafts), people normally like to spread out from each other. They prefer an empty seat to one that is partially occupied. Also, people tend to sit next to other people with whom they identify. Old people sit with old people, blacks sit with blacks, hippies sit with hippies. The primary division, however, is between male and female. (Once in a while you may get a racial crossover, such as a black woman who prefers to sit next to a black man rather than a white woman.) You can watch a white middle-aged man board a bus full of housewives and walk down a double row of prospective seats so he can sit next to another white middle-aged man.

But if that same man walks clear to the other end of the bus, passing vacant seats, to sit next to a pretty young girl, his motives may be questionable. If the girl starts looking uneasy and embarrassed, it may be that she needs help. Go back there and stand over the man. If nothing is going on, he probably won't even notice you. If he was molesting her, he will probably be intimidated by your presence and stop. If you actually catch him in the act, you should notify the driver and have him apprehended.

It has become all too common for young girls to be sexually accosted before they reach puberty. In any civilized society, the young must be protected. Women have to become concerned with their sisters, at least to the point of protecting those who are not yet psychologically able to fend for themselves. While learning to protect themselves, women must also recognize the necessity of protecting each other.

If you have to wait on a dark train platform, it may be better to wait near the cashier's booth. If that isn't possible, stay under a light, and close to any other woman waiting for the train. Be aware of any male who "accidentally" wanders close enough to make you feel uneasy. People rarely venture into the personal space of a complete stranger without some intent. What's uncomfortably close for you will normally be uncomfortably close for someone else. Again, look alert rather than pretending that there is no cause for concern. Use the same precautions that would apply to walking on the street.

If you're driving through a dangerous neighborhood, of course you should have your doors locked and the windows rolled up. Don't ever park your car where you wouldn't otherwise walk. If you have to, break down and spend the money for a parking lot.

If you see a woman hitchhiking, stop and pick her up. There's no great inconvenience to you, and it could spare her a lot of trouble. If you are the woman hitchhiking, you should know better. It's your decision, of course, but hitchhiking is a *very* high-risk activity.

If you have to use an elevator at night, avoid getting on one occupied solely by a man. Wait for the next elevator. If you both enter at the same time or you don't feel like waiting, stand by the controls and ask him for his floor before you punch yours. Stay near the control buttons. Elevator etiquette demands that passengers keep a distance and avoid looking at each other. Be aware of any encroachments on your space.

The matter of defending yourself against acquaintances can't be put into such clear-cut terms. It is fairly easy to keep strangers out of your life. Acquaintances are a much more delicate problem.

Of the case histories we've examined, less than half of the victims fall prey to a perfect stranger. The majority were attacked, not by close friends, but by acquaintances or friends of friends.

The particular acquaintance who may be a problem is easy enough to identify: he's either the man who treats you much more as a chick than as a person, or the man who seems to bear some sort of grudge against you. A difficulty arises when a woman knows a man slightly: enough to trust him somewhat, but not enough to know if he's to be trusted. Perhaps he's in some of your classes. Perhaps he's your new boss. Perhaps he's someone you know only by reputation. Whatever the case, he's generally someone with whom you want to be on good terms. Your ego could use an enviable boy friend. Your boss could make things unpleasant for you. And so you let yourself be pushed into a situation you know to be dangerous. Later you may blame yourself for being so naïve.

A certain alarm goes off in your mind when you realize that you're not in a position that's easy to defend, or that the man is pushing you just a little too hard. You may ignore your inner warning because you don't want to seem concerned or look foolish. But he knows he's maneuvering you, and plays off your feigned nonchalance. You like to think you can always outsmart him. Or perhaps you reassure yourself that you can charm your way out of anything. It's a shame it doesn't work. You have to be blunt, make a stand, perhaps even look foolish. You will undoubtedly lose a suitor, which in this case would be no loss. Here, the only person you are trying to impress is the man who is intimidating you. And you don't have a chance of impressing him.

As we've pointed out previously, once you start to play along with the situation, you're trapped. The point is not to start, to stay clear of the entire matter. Once you know a man fairly well, you can tell if he represents any potential trouble. If you don't know him that well, stay out of any unusual situations with him.

The highest risk among acquaintances seems to be the friends or relatives of someone you already know. The person you know introduces you, and you treat the second man with much the same familiarity with which you would treat your friend. Then the acquaintance maneuvers the mutual friend out of the way, and you find yourself very much alone with this man, whom you really don't know at all. At this point you may be in a great deal of trouble. If you don't know a man very well, stay out of any unusual situations with him.

Another particularly hazardous group is men who are of a different social, economic, racial, or ethnic background. Saying this may not do much for the sake of world peace, but you have to recognize that there is a lot of hostility between different groups and it's up to you to stay out of the line of fire.

A man from a different group may well have you classified as "that kind" of woman. Part of the stereotype of any group defined as inferior is that the men are shiftless and the women are sluts. Whites use that on black people, straights use that on hippies, wealthy people use that on poor people. Americans use that on Vietnamese. There is also the factor that the man may consider only the people of his own group as real human beings, which makes it much easier to classify you.

The precautions we've recommended so far are all for use against outsiders. But you may also have to deal with a rape by someone close to you—your husband, lover, ex-husband, or ex-lover. In such situations, you certainly can't rely on keeping this person out of your life. But you should know this man well enough to recognize when he's inclined to become insistent and violent. It is reported that most murdered women are killed by angry husbands or lovers. Surely these women had some warning that their men were capable of hurting them.

We aren't suggesting that your man will rape you, or that you should leave him to be sure that he won't rape you. But if he's ever treated you violently or with contempt, it's only sane that you should act with caution. You should also question whether or not you really want to be involved with this man.

While precaution is the best defense, it may not invariably be practical and possible. There may be times when the man has pushed the situation beyond the point of avoidance, and you may have to resort to more direct measures, such as physical self-defense. Some people, reading over our advice, will say that it verges on paranoia. Actually, we have tried to screen out any suggestions that were too demanding. But paranoia is a necessary part of survival. When you consider our society, paranoia is to be expected. You shouldn't be ashamed of it, or try to deny it, but, rather, you should deal with it.

Instead of convincing yourself that paranoia is unhealthy, take positive action to ease your mind. Have something big and mean to grab on to, like a sharp metal box next to your bed. Maybe it won't do you much good if someone, somehow, breaks in, but it will make you feel better if you hear sounds in the night.

Decide that your home is your own territory, and that any intruder who comes in when you're around will find himself in a very bad fix. Arrange your house so that you feel it's impossible for someone to come in without causing an uproar. If you come in at night by yourself and you feel afraid, yell "Hey." Then wait before going in farther. Give anyone who doesn't want to be caught a chance to get away. This is suggested as more of a cure for paranoia than as a way of scaring intruders. If you have any reason to feel afraid—and your apartment should be secure enough so that this is not an every-night fear—go to a neighbor or call a friend and don't enter the apartment until you have company. Most important, don't feel silly about being afraid when you have a reason to be, even if the reason is that something simply *feels* wrong.

Carrying some sort of weapon when you go out is very good for paranoia. It is something to back you up if you ever need it. It might also give you the self-confidence to stand up to a man who is bothering you. You should of course take stock of the situation before you start asserting yourself, but if you feel secure, let him have it. When enough women do this, things will start to change.

PRECAUTIONS TO KEEP IN MIND

On the street

Be familiar with your own limitations.

Be familiar with your own frequently used route. (Look at it through new eyes—notice lighting, alleys, abandoned buildings, and street people.)

Have a place you consider safe if you feel you are being followed—a place where you could either make a stand or reassure yourself that you are not being followed.

If you come home late, vary your route.

Carrying Mace is recommended while you are walking, but we suggest that a road flare be carried in your car. You drive many places you would never consider going on foot, and a road flare will get you out of almost anything.

Whatever you carry, be familiar with it. Practice using it a few times before you start carrying it. You'll feel better.

Always carry enough money for an emergency whenever you go out.

Develop a way of carrying your weapon so that it won't be forgotten at home. Leave it in a jacket pocket or on your belt.

Dress sanely.

While waiting for public transportation, keep your back against a wall.

If you're going somewhere in a city you aren't familiar with, check a map. Know where you're going and don't look lost.

In large parking lots, write down your position so you can go straight back to your car.

Look in your back seat before you get into the car.

Try to use the Laundromat in the daytime or early evening.

Use a grocery cart for laundry or many packages. You make a good mark when your arms are full.

Apartment living

A person with a key in his hand does not necessarily live in your building. Be a lady and wait until he opens the front door.

If a man is coming into the building behind you, pull the locked front door shut after you enter, even if it will be obvious to him that you are shutting him out. He'll understand, or, if he doesn't, you were justified.

A visitor who has "just rung the buzzer" should be allowed to wait to see if his friend is home.

Once you open your door, go inside immediately. Don't leave it half open.

If you live in an elevator building, before you step on the elevator make sure it has not been summoned to the roof or the basement.

Don't get on an elevator occupied solely by a man. If there are other passengers who get off the elevator, except for one man you don't know, get off with them and wait for another car. If you are alone on the elevator and a strange man (or a group of men) gets on and you feel uncomfortable, get off. Manually controlled elevators are without a doubt a difficult part of maintaining personal safety. Use your judgment.

You can force your landlord to install a good lock.

It is preferable to have a dead-bolt lock, and a chain, as well as a peephole.

Window locks should be set so that there isn't room for even a small child to crawl through.

There may be a statute allowing you to keep a dog for protection even though your lease doesn't permit it. Check for yourself.

When you have safeguarded your home, go outside and see if there isn't some way you can break in.

Do your best to bring your life back to the way you *want* to live.

"If a guy grabs you, scream," says [*Chicago police sergeant*] *Sandburg.* *"If he's got a knife at your throat or a gun at your head, relax and enjoy it."*
Terri Schultz, "Rape, Fear, and the Law"

CHAPTER SEVEN

Self-Defense

It was late at night in a New York subway. A tall blond woman was on her way home from a consciousness-raising session, having spent several hours talking about being harassed on the street. At the meeting she had found herself getting angry, but the anger had been exhilarating to her. Behind a post stood a small, middle-aged man. As she went past, he made kissing noises at her. She stopped, turned around, and walked over to the man. She looked down at him.

"Did you say something?"

"What? No, I didn't say anything."

"I think you did. I think you made a funny noise, like this." And she demonstrated.

"Oh, that."

"Yes, that. Do you do that often?"

"Only when a pretty girl goes by."

"Oh, only when a pretty girl goes by. Well, do you know what? I don't like it. I don't consider it a compliment. And if I ever catch you doing it again, to me or to any of my sisters, I'm going to beat the living daylights out of you."

The sidewalks were crowded as Polly headed toward her office in the Chicago Loop. There was a man who had been close to her elbow for about half a block, but after all it was awfully crowded. Then the man moved in closer and said, "Hey, baby, wanna go have a drink?"

"Why you goddamned bastard!" she said, as she swung her heavy shoulder bag at him, hitting him square across the back. "You ought to be ashamed of yourself."

He turned to flee, and she, changing direction, followed him, yelling at the top of her lungs, "A wedding band on your finger and you go down the street propositioning innocent women. What would your wife have to say about that!

"You creep, you. You've got some nerve to bother women on the street when you've got a wife at home," she continued as people in the street stopped dead in their tracks. There were various looks of shock and surprise; some of the men looked worried.

On the Chicago el trains there is a narrow space between the end of the seat and the side of the car. It isn't much of a space, just about wide enough for a man's hand. A woman of indeterminate age, perhaps twenty, perhaps thirty, was sitting near the window. In her hand was a large book, which she kept closed. Then, through the space, from the seat behind, a man's hand appeared. It came to rest on her breast. The book rose out of her lap, smashed the hand into the wall, and went back to her lap. The man in the seat in back of her howled with pain, and got off at the next stop.

There was a long wait to see the doctor that night. One woman, attractive, curly-haired, and in Chicago only a few weeks since leaving Oklahoma, was feeling uncomfortable sitting in the waiting room. The town and the neighborhood both seemed strange to her and there wasn't anyone to talk to. Suddenly a scream came from the street. No one moved, but a few women looked up. The scream came again. The young woman jumped out of her chair and ran into the street. She saw a man with a beer bottle, about to smash it into the face of a prostrate woman. Our heroine ran over, kicked the man in the groin, and knocked him down. As he climbed to his feet, two people grabbed him from behind and dragged him off. The woman returned to the waiting room, sat down, and shook.

A very small, young, and innocent-looking woman was walking down an empty street at night. Blue-eyed, blond-haired, she looked cherubic. She certainly didn't look like a karate teacher.

An annoying man in a car apparently didn't consider her formidable-looking. He was slowly cruising alongside her, calling out the window and making suggestions. She didn't respond. Finally, he got out of the car, grabbed her by the arm, and pulled her toward the waiting auto. She spun, snapped a kick into his groin, and put her knee into his face as he bent forward. She held her stance and waited to see what he would do. He staggered back to his car. She went on with her walk.

Standing up and fighting back. Stories like the ones above, all true, make you feel a little prouder, a little stronger, knowing that somewhere there are women who have won.

It's a good feeling, but any woman knows that victories like these don't come easily. The women in these stories were, respectively: big, on a crowded street, original, damned lucky, and highly trained. All of them were strong, effective women.

Defending ourselves and other women isn't a matter to be taken lightly, on a wave of enthusiasm and blinding optimism. Those are unreal feelings for what could well be an ugly reality. And they aren't feelings that will work in a crisis; in that kind of situation, you have to rely on your instinct for survival, your self-determination and self-respect, and you must have the basic belief that you're worth fighting for.

Perhaps the first thing you have to think about is the amount of abuse you're willing to take before fighting back. You have to decide the value you place on yourself, and the value you place on others, especially men. Again and again women have explained to us that they didn't use available weapons against their attackers because they were afraid they would hurt them. They had clearly met with disbelief when they admitted this to other people, and this led to a confusion on their parts which sometimes lasted for years. It isn't hard to appreciate their problem. If you don't understand a situation, if you've never fought back before, if you don't know how it will affect you, it's going to be difficult to grab the lamp from the bedside table and bring it crashing down on the man's head.

One of the subtle limitations we face as women is the prejudice that a woman is incapable of effective violence. Lady wrestlers are freaks; cat fights funny. A woman fighting a man is Jane beating her fists against Tarzan's chest. People say that a woman will only get hurt struggling against a man. That's true. Struggling will only get the woman injured; fighting may work.

In an all-out fight between an average, untrained man and an average, untrained woman at close quarters, the man will win, to be sure. But a rape situation isn't necessarily going to be like that. You should be educated to maneuver the situation to your own best advantage, and to take any possible opportunity to escape.

The key here is that a rape attack will not necessarily be an all-out fight. The objective is not to beat your opponent, but to surprise him by resisting and then to take the opportunity to flee. An attempt to fight off the attacker may result in your getting hit or injured—this is something you have to expect and prepare for. If you kick your attacker, then find yourself being punched in return and give up at the sign of the slightest injury, you may just as well not have fought at all. Because women have not had much experience in fights (wrestling, football, any contact sport), they tend to think that they must give up before the real fighting begins. Be prepared. This is not a game. You must be ready for a blow, take it, and then go on. It's the fear of being struck that is paralyzing, not the reality. In a confrontation you probably won't be aware of any injury until it's all over with and you are recovering your senses.

If the situation actually is hopeless, of course, you'll always have the option of giving up. But surrendering doesn't guarantee that you won't be hurt. At the very least, you'll be raped, and he may hurt you further. In a violent confrontation with a rapist, there is no easy way out. But if it is practical to fight, you should know how to fight effectively.

Somehow the concept seems unreal, even upsetting to some people. A police sergeant advised women against carrying guns or knives to protect themselves; instead he suggested carrying hatpins. His rationale was that an assailant might take the weapon from her and use it against her. It is true that the woman will probably be hurt resisting in this way if she is so incompetent in the use of a knife that the man can take it from her, or if she doesn't have the will to use the knife against him because it might hurt him. In any case, if the man is so overpowering that he can disarm her, he won't need her knife to hurt her. But if the woman seriously means to defend herself against an opponent, and she's depending on her weapon, she surely shouldn't be fending him off with a three-inch piece of wire. The thought of a man defending himself against a robber with a hatpin is absurd. The only reason the thought isn't equally absurd when applied to a woman is that we have been taught to think of women as ineffectual.

Both men and women seem to be threatened by the idea of a woman who can fight, even if she fights a rapist. To men, while it's certainly honorable for a man to be capable of defending a woman's honor, it's threatening for her to be capable of defending it by herself. Or defending herself against him, should the need ever arise. There's a strange fear that if women ever learn to fight, every man would be in imminent danger, which may say something about the guilt of the ruling class. The idea is preposterous. Have there ever been bands of women roaming the streets, terrorizing citizens? Or groups of women having shoot-outs with the law? Or drunken women picking fights with random men?

Women have their own hang-ups against fighting back. They may fear that if they ever let go, they'd kill the man. They are overestimating themselves. People aren't that easy to kill, and they are fighting for a chance to escape, not to murder. Men are rarely killed with a single blow, and if what a woman does to him is seriously damaging, he'll be glad to let her go. Women fear their own anger because, since they've never seriously struck someone in anger, they've never learned what happens when they do.

It's a good idea to learn to think out a situation in terms of action and cool-headed practicality. You may well have a great deal of time to think about it. It's rare that a rapist suddenly leaps from the shadows. Even when the man's a stranger, there's usually a preliminary encounter before the attack, while he builds himself up to committing violence. You should be able to sense the hostility. Check out your surroundings and be aware of what may be coming. Of course you should try to avoid the whole confrontation; you've learned more about handling men during your adolescence than we could ever put in a book.

Once you know that an attack is imminent, scream. That sounds like an obvious instruction, but you'd be surprised how many women have never screamed in their lives. (Try it some time, just for practice.) It will clear your head, start the adrenaline going, perhaps scare off the attacker, and it might even summon help. When you scream, make sure that anyone listening understands that you want help. There are a number of people who might rush to your aid if they hear you calling, "Help, call the police, rape," but who would stay away if they hear, "Get away from me, leave me alone." In the first case it is clear what is happening; in the second, you could be having an argument with a friend and a passer-by would be loath to get involved.

If you can't avoid the rapist's attack, at least you can work against his maneuvers and set up the confrontation to your own best advantage. Concentrate on his weaknesses. He has to get close to you. He feels pain. He's afraid of feeling pain. And he's afraid of getting caught. You can exploit his weaknesses, if only enough to make him lose the confidence he needs as the aggressor and thus give you a chance to escape.

Physically he also has certain weak points you can exploit. The human body is very poorly designed, with its tottering posture, S-shaped spine, and wobbly knees. There are a number of vulnerable points on any human, especially on the front of the body. When our predecessors were down on all fours, it was practical to have the back well protected by muscle and bone, with the vulnerable points on the underbelly; the only part left exposed was the face, which was protected by the teeth. When people pulled themselves up on two legs and lost their more fearsome teeth, a good deal was left open.

Don't underestimate your attacker, of course. He wouldn't be confronting you if he didn't think he could handle you. But he may be overestimating himself. Perhaps he's a scrawny fifteen-year-old, or an ordinary man who simply doesn't expect any resistance. These are considerations to keep in mind.

You have certain advantages in being on the defensive. It's up to you to keep him back and avoid as much fighting as possible. The less involved you are in the fight, the less likely you are to get hurt. You have one objective, and that's to end the encounter; either to leave, or to make him leave. Another possible advantage is the degree of the rapist's determination. When we asked about the rapist's attitude on our questionnaire, a large number of women described it as matter-of-fact. In other words, he expects you to go along with him. It's possible that you can show him that you want *not* to be raped much more than he wants to rape you. In some cases, serious resistance may be enough to discourage him.

On the other hand, it may not. The man, the situation, and your own personality are the determining factors in any confrontation. At best, we can offer suggestions that should be practical in potential situations. No one knows quite what you may encounter, and we can't know how you tend to react. So anything we suggest should be tempered by your own viewpoint and common sense. What we present here are simply some basic suggestions designed for reasonably capable but untrained women. We've tried to avoid any that are complicated or impractical. What we present requires a minimum of practice, but it does require practice. And it should be practiced with another person.

Who you practice with is important. When you're first sorting things out, it's better to work with another woman, one you feel at ease with, so you can settle your mutual problems. Then, if possible, you might want to find a big, heavy man to practice with. But at all times, keep it clear in your mind that you're working together to help each other. You don't want a female partner who will tell you flatly, "Well, that's nice, but what if he hits you with a brick?" or a big man who paternally demonstrates how much weaker you are. You don't need any more undermining. Psychologically, these people are preparing you to lose. Prepare to win. If someone gets you into a hold you can't break, work to discover what can be done. If nothing else, you should come to realize the importance of keeping someone from grabbing you.

After every practice, you should be able to leave feeling a little more confident and able to cope—you've just been teaching yourself to be better prepared. If you leave feeling less competent than when you began, something is very wrong.

It's also important to prepare yourself mentally. Imagine an attack, and think about what you would do to escape. But think positively. After everyone else has told you that you'll fail at defending yourself, you hardly want to tell yourself the same.

In any case, we'd like you to remember that nothing we suggest is magic. Karate isn't magic, nor is kung fu, nor is anything else. You may kick someone in the knee only to find that he has a wooden leg. While every maneuver is practical, there is always the possibility it may not work. So always provide another tactic as a stand-by. First, keep strangers at a certain distance; if you can't keep them away entirely, keep them from making contact with you. Scream. If they manage to grab you anyway, break away; if you can't break away, immediately attack; if you can't attack, wait and see what can be done. There's no way of predicting exactly what may happen or what may work. Much depends on chance. But you can learn to manipu-

late chance, if you first take control of your own life and surroundings.

The suggestions in this chapter are no substitute for a good course
in self-defense. Systematic training of your body will leave you much
better prepared than our suggestions alone can do. We know, unfortunately, that it's impossible for every woman who reads this book to
join a class in self-defense; effective courses for women are still rare.
Any decent course should prepare you to cope in a practical situation. Too many women recognize that their self-defense course is
impractical, but accept it for lack of anything better. If you can't
develop a fairly realistic self-defense course (and it's for you as well
as the teacher to make the class realistic), try karate. For a woman, a
good self-defense course, incorporating the essentials of street fighting, is better than a karate course. But even a poor karate course is
better than a poor self-defense course.

We recommend karate rather than the other Oriental military arts.
Judo is essentially a sport and will bring you much too close to a
dangerous opponent. Aikido, while effective, is more difficult to
master.

However, all the Oriental martial forms were designed for males
fighting several hundred years ago, and they've been considerably
ritualized since. Even karate isn't completely relevant to a woman
who's mainly interested in surviving in contemporary America. But
there are certain things to be gained from it. Your endurance and
general well-being will improve, your reflexes will sharpen, and you'll
develop automatic reactions.

The following sections are intended as a practical working guide to
self-defense. We will start with the most basic problems—how to
stand, how to stay on your feet, how to avoid a blow—and then
advance to more active measures—kicks, hand strikes, and weapons.
Each of these steps should be practiced, with the book nearby for
quick reference to the diagrams. Using these basic instructions, you
can then expand your practice sessions. Experiment with your stance.
Get involved in it. Use your body until you begin to know it better.
Learn your weaknesses and find out how to improve them, or work
around them. If you can't work with someone, at least read through
this section. It will give you some ideas that might be of help to you if
you are attacked.

Stance

For an untrained woman we recommend standing with feet widely spread, one in front of the other, as if you were walking. Don't spread your legs so far that you feel off balance. You want a solid base. The front foot is pointed forward, the rear foot is either pointed forward or out, whichever is more comfortable. Your forward leg is bent at the knee and flexible; your rear leg is straight, acting as a brace. Your arms are up to protect your vulnerable points. One arm is forward and bent at the elbow, so that the fist is even with the face, protecting your head and body. The other fist is alongside your waist.

Keep head up; watch opponent

Arm in "high block" position

Straight back

Body centered and balanced on hips

Bend front knee

Rear leg straight

Point front foot forward

Don't spread feet too far apart

Point foot either forward or outward

Your back should be straight, and you should feel that your body is well balanced on your hips. This stance is designed so that you're well protected, well balanced, and able to lash out without leaving yourself too vulnerable. Have your partner push and pull you, to make sure that you are standing solidly.

When you move in this position, don't use walking or running movements—they leave you off balance. Either leap or slide. Both are much smoother and faster.

You should practice this stance until you become completely accustomed to it, so that you fall into it whenever you trip or lose your balance. It's a good idea to practice it while standing on a bus or subway, trying to keep your balance without holding on to anything.

When practicing for a fighting situation, your hands should always be up and ready to block. Even when you're using your hands to attack, you should always have one arm up to defend yourself. Protecting yourself is much more important than hitting someone else.

Drop into your stance when you think it is necessary. If you don't want to look suspicious, merely stand upright with your hands out of your pockets and have your feet in position.

If a man tries to grab you or strike you

The best way to deal with any grab or punch is to deflect the man's arm before it reaches you. Make a fist and hold your arm out a foot or so parallel to your body, with your fist at eye level. Sweep your arm in front of your body, from side to side, so that you could deflect any punch or grab to your head or upper body. Practice sweeping up and down as well as side to side, keeping your fist an even twelve inches from your body. Don't try to grab his hands. Simply knock them away from you. Here speed is essential. Have your partner try to get past your defenses.

Kicks

As an offensive tactic, it's best for a woman to rely on kicking. A man will be likely to grab for you or perhaps punch, but your kick is longer than his reach. Your legs are also the strongest part of your body—they've been carrying your weight for your entire lifetime.

To kick from your stance, you should bring your rear leg up and forward, and hold your leg up, bent sharply at the knee, so that you're standing like a stork. Now snap your kick out from the knee. Go back into the stork position, and put your foot back behind you. It's very important that your kick snaps out from your knee. If you kick with a straight leg, you lose force and throw yourself badly off balance. Try a few fairly high kicks. If you feel like you're leaning backward, you're not bending your knee enough. Practice kicking from your stance, then going directly back into your stance and kicking again. Keep it up. It will give you a good feeling for the power and balance of your kick and stance.

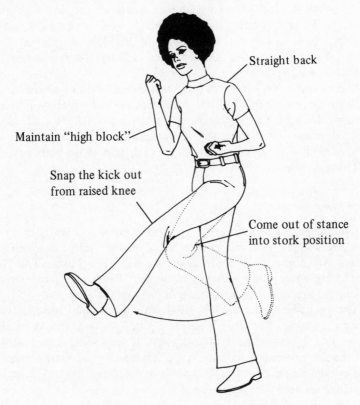

Straight back

Maintain "high block"

Snap the kick out
from raised knee

Come out of stance
into stork position

Besides actually disabling someone, kicks are also useful in keeping your attacker away from you. If your kick is longer than his reach (and it should be), a barrage of fast, sharp kicks should be enough to keep him at bay. But remember, always kick with your rear foot. For practice, put an object on the floor and see how close you would have to be to kick it with your front foot. Now kick it with your rear foot—you will be able to strike well beyond it.

Practice your kicks with your shoes on. You'll probably be wearing shoes if attacked. Kick your opponent with the toe of your shoe. If you spend a lot of time barefoot or wearing sandals, you should learn to kick with the ball of your foot. Otherwise you would hurt your toes.

Your best target is his knee: it's low, difficult to protect, and easily knocked out of place. The kneecap isn't securely attached, and a kick up under it, or a glancing kick across it, is likely to knock it out of position. In any case, it is painful, if not disabling. A glancing kick across the kneecap is the most effective kick we can recommend to untrained women.

Unless you're very fast, we don't recommend kicking to the groin. A man naturally protects the groin, and he may grab your foot, perhaps throwing you off balance. A kick to the shin is easily done and will cause him sharp pain but no real disability. However, if he's in a vulnerable position, a solid kick to any part of his body or head will have an effect.

Using your hands

Other types of kicks begin to get complicated, so we'll go on to hand techniques. Here we can get a little more varied, as untrained people will normally be more dexterous with their hands. The kick should be your primary means of attack. Don't use hand strikes unless you are unable to jump back, or he lunges in after you.

The basic fist is a clenched hand with the thumb outside, lying along the fingers. The wrist is absolutely straight; you should be able to lay a pencil on the back of your wrist. If your wrist is bent, it will only buckle on contact. Aim with the first knuckles of your forefinger and middle finger (the knuckles at the base of the fingers). Imagine punching through your opponent.

The basic punch begins with your fist alongside your waist, thumb-side up. Your other arm protects your body. The fist comes up and out, and has a turn in mid-air, so that you strike thumbside down. This adds extra force to your blow.

While the basic punching form remains the same, you don't always want to strike with the basic fist. In fact, that might be the least effective way. The force would be more concentrated if you used a half fist, with your hand only partially closed and contact made with the second set of knuckles. Keep your wrist in a straight line with your knuckles.

Now you must choose a target. Your opponent has a number of vulnerable points on the upper part of his body. If he's wearing a coat, or if he has a generally heavy build, don't try any blows to the torso—he'll be able to absorb them with relatively little effect. Aim instead for the head and throat.

You might also try a blow to a soft point with a spear-shaped hand. Here you hold your hand flat and tensed, and make contact with fingertips. Keep your fingers bent slightly inward, so that if you do strike something hard, your fingers won't bend backward.

If the man has rushed you, however, you may not have room for a punch. While a short jab with a spear hand would be effective, there are other things to do at close quarters. The following blows should be combined with each other, so that if you hit a man once, you can hit him again on the backhand and get in a series of strikes. If he is this close, you want a maximum effect. Concentrate on his head and throat.

A flat-hand blow would be caused by using the heel of the palm to slam into the side of his temple, or into his ear. A blow to the temple will damage the blood supply to the brain, and may disorient or stun him. A blow to the ear may upset his balance or rupture his eardrum. A knife hand is the good old James Bond karate chop. Hold your hand as with the spear hand, but strike with the side of the hand; don't hit with the side of your fingers.

If you're very close to him, you can hit him with the heel of your palm, coming up under his chin or under his nose. If there is a wall in back of him, try slamming his head up and back against it. A sharp poke to the hollow of the throat will have an effect. The trachea is quite close to the surface at that point, and by pressing you can cut off his air. In an emergency, jab hard. If you want to try a poke to the eyes, come up from below so he doesn't see you.

You can also try coming down from above and clawing at his eyes. Unless you are very fast, you probably won't make contact with the eyes themselves. You'll just tear off his glasses or lacerate his eyelids. It'll probably frighten him more than anything else, but don't try it unless you feel warranted in blinding him.

General suggestions

With these overall techniques to refer to, we are ready to talk about what to do if you are attacked. We have a few general suggestions.

When walking down the street, keep your hands out of your pockets. If you sense a confrontation coming on, maneuver so that you can control the location. (Don't feel foolish about running away. Run first—you can decide about foolishness later.) If you carry a police whistle, you should blow it as soon as you feel threatened. If you have anything that can be used as a weapon, you should have it out by now. Choose as open a place as possible, with you standing on even, solid ground. If at all possible, avoid ice and snow.

Keep an avenue of escape in mind.

Concentrate on being calm and rational.

Keep him as far back as possible.

Watch his eyes while keeping his arms in your peripheral vision. Most people will glance at their target before they strike.

It's very important to stay upright and on your feet. You can use your speed and agility to advantage against his size and strength only so long as he doesn't trap you. Stay out of any wrestling matches. Try to react with speed rather than form. When you strike, use a strong, bellowing war cry.

Have one reaction for any emergency. (We recommend a high block. See illustration, page 81.) If you have an automatic response, it will keep you from freezing. A high block may not always be appropriate, but a confrontation is so rapid and so confusing that you won't have time to decide what you *should* do until it's all over. Any strong reaction will be likely to confuse your attacker, and at least keep you from being an easy target.

Use blows in combination with each other.

Once you hit him somewhere effectively, keep striking to the same point, with enough variation to confuse him. If it hurt the first time, it will be much worse the second, third, and fourth times.

Don't ever expect a single blow to end the fight.

If one thing doesn't work, immediately try something else.

Recognizing danger

In almost any attack there will be some kind of hostility before the attacker gets violent. If you are street-wise, you can recognize the routine easily enough: the jostling for position is usually obvious. Even if you're not familiar with it, you'll probably be feeling distinctly uneasy and sense that there is trouble coming. We only ask you to listen to your intuition.

The man may make overtly threatening statements. You may be too frightened to return the hostility, but don't try to chase him away by claiming to have a black belt in karate or some such thing. He's not going to believe you, and will only take it as a challenge. (Of course, if you do have a black belt, you can say anything you like.) Don't try to tell him about your skill in self-defense, or that you're carrying Mace. Whatever you have in your favor, let it be a surprise to him. It can be to your advantage for him to consider you a poor, helpless female, just as long as you remember that you're not poor and helpless. It's rarely advisable to make a threat that you can't enforce.

If you resist, your attacker may try to bargain with you. Don't believe him. It's a standard game: if he can get you to comply with one thing, it's much easier to get you to comply with the next thing.

Breaking a hold

The above are simply common-sense suggestions that you should always keep in mind. Now, if a man has gotten close to you and he lays his hands on you, there are certain ways of getting them off. We also have some suggestions for hold-breaking.

The faster and more abruptly you react, the better. If you break his hold before he has a firm grip on you, it's more likely that you'll get away. Also, the longer he has a hold on you, the weaker your muscles will become from lack of circulation.

If you try to break away and you find you can't, immediately attack before he expects it.

If you can't break away at first, wait until he doesn't expect it. A typical pattern would be for him to grab you and say something. There is a pause. You reply. Pause. You try to break. Instead, look at him while he's talking and break in the middle of his sentence.

If you're being choked, it's essential to deal with *that* immediately. You lose your muscle strength in a surprisingly short time if your oxygen has been cut off.

Please don't expect things to happen like a textbook pattern. There will be all sorts of variations.

We'll deal with holds from the front first. If a man is choking you from the front, he'll have a grip on your neck with his hands. Pry up his little fingers and wrench them backward, trying to break them. If you break or dislocate them, the pain will be too great for him to use his hands.

If he grabs you with his body flat against yours, you won't be able to free your arms. Suddenly throw your weight to one side—for him to keep his balance, he'll have to spread his legs; snap your knee into his groin.

If possible in this sort of situation, have your arms pinned up against your body rather than alongside. If your fists are up against your chest, you can move with a blow to his head or throat when he begins to let go of you. Your arms are of no use alongside your body.

If a man grabs your wrist, it is not as threatening as a choke, but it is clear he has something in mind. You should concentrate your force against his thumb, which is the weakest part of his grip. If he's too strong, or if he's twisting your wrist, grab your captured hand with your free hand and throw all your weight into breaking his grip. These moves in particular should be done rapidly.

If a man grabs you from behind, it is either to choke you into submission or to drag you somewhere. If he was going to hit you from behind, he would have done so already. Don't let him pull you off your feet—jump with him and use him to support yourself.

If you feel yourself being grabbed from behind in any way, throw a rear block. Have one arm up as in a high block; then pivot and forcefully turn around. Pivot as hard as you can and throw your whole weight into the block. This should suffice to break his hold if he is holding you at a distance (say, to avoid getting kicked or elbowed).

If you can't turn around, it means that he's flat against you, and you should launch into a different attack.

In this case, you're not going to be able to break out of his hold; you'll have to make things unpleasant enough for him to make him release you. Which isn't that hard. Your back is well protected, and he's too close to hit you effectively. At the same time, the front of his body is open to your attack.

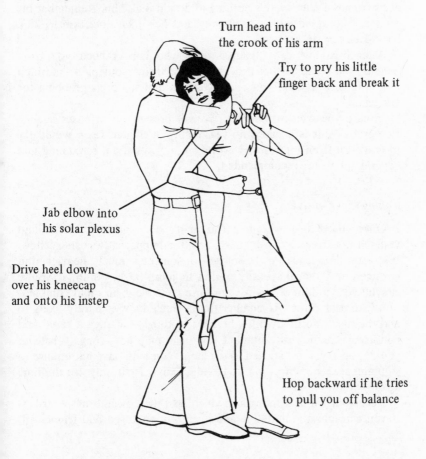

Turn head into the crook of his arm

Try to pry his little finger back and break it

Jab elbow into his solar plexus

Drive heel down over his kneecap and onto his instep

Hop backward if he tries to pull you off balance

Bring your heel down over his kneecap and attempt to drive it down his leg. Drive your heel down his shin and slam it into his instep. Keep it up. Concentrate on the kneecap instead of his instep; he might be wearing boots. Whenever you use your feet, look down and aim.

Jab your elbow into his solar plexus. This may not have much effect in the wintertime when you're both wearing heavy coats, but it may do some good anyway.

If the man is choking you with his forearm, immediately turn your throat into the crook of his elbow. It may still hurt, but you'll be able to breathe. Then proceed to stomp him. If a man has pinned your arms from the rear, there's nothing to do but kick him. Remember his arms are occupied with you already and he's in no position to kick back. Just stay on your feet.

After breaking away from a man who has grabbed you from behind, you should either run like hell or throw your pivot and high block. If he's grabbed you once, you can anticipate his grabbing for you again.

In case you were wondering, we will present no defenses against side grabs. This is because no reasonably intelligent felon would try to grab you from the side. However, in any situation, screaming and general uproar are recommended.

Taking the offensive

Once you've broken out of this man's hold, however, you'll find yourself in extremely close quarters with an apparently hostile fellow. It's very dangerous to be close to someone much heavier and stronger, so if you have any option to jump back, do so. If you're caught close to him or against him, use your blows in rapid combination with each other. Remember that a single blow is hardly likely to end the fight. You may miss, he may be tough—in such a rapid and confusing situation any number of things may go wrong. Whatever you do, once you get started, don't stop. You may have an impulse to stop and see what effect you're having. Don't. He'll only use the time against you.

Accustom yourself to strikes which lead directly into more strikes. If you can take the initiative and keep *him* confused and frightened, you may well be able to discourage him even if you don't land any solid, serious blows. Of course, that doesn't mean you should restrain yourself; you're in a grave confrontation, and if you're going to fight, fight to win.

A trick that may help would be to take advantage of a time when he is close to you and bent forward for some reason (say, to block a kick). Grab his hair or the top of his head, and bring your weight down on him, as if you were slamming a trunk. Double him up, and if appropriate, knee him in the face. Whatever happens, once you have him doubled up, keep him down. If he gives you any trouble at all, knee him. Walk him over to unlock the door, or walk him to a busy street; don't let him up until you're sure you're safe. If he does somehow roll out of your grip (which would be difficult), either run or kick him before he can get to his feet again.

Weapons

Even though we have suggested any number of unarmed defenses, you'd be better off carrying a weapon of sorts for emergencies. Presently there are a number of spray Mace devices which are essentially aerosol tear gas. While we recommend Mace, please remember that it isn't magic, any more than karate or self-defense. Mace is very easily carried in a jacket pocket, and may be psychologically as easy to use as Raid. But there are problems involved. You have to spray into the man's face, which would involve being close, facing him, and having an arm free. In a high wind you may be affected as well. And there's the matter that Mace is illegal in many states. But it does have definite advantages as it takes no particular skill to use, is so convenient that you can always have it with you, and, as with any weapon, is something to hang on to in an emergency.

If you are more old-fashioned, and carry something like a knife, we certainly hope you know how to use it. Please don't go around with a Boy Scout knife buried somewhere in the bottom of your purse. Carrying a handgun would probably protect you, but we feel that it's much more important that there be tighter gun control in this country and that no one but police be allowed to carry handguns. Women can only gain in this war by de-escalating.

Another recommendation we have already made is that you carry a road flare in your car, or with you, if you are going somewhere particularly unsafe. Essentially, this device is a compact flame thrower. It has a two-to-three-inch flame, can be used to flick burning sulfur for approximately seven feet, and is blinding to your opponent. You should be sure to keep your own eyes shielded from the glare, and to sweep it in front of you to maintain a barricade of fire. Your attacker will keep his eyes on it as long as you keep it moving. It's also likely to bring help. Remember that a flare can be lit only by striking against the cap; you should be sure that the wick never gets dirty or battered, or it won't light.

While a flare is the most effective weapon for an untrained person, it is rather awkward to carry with you. If you want something to leave in your pocket and forget about, Mace would be the answer. Once you are in a bad neighborhood, you can be forced out of your car.

If you find yourself unprepared in a threatening situation, there are all sorts of things which make fine impromptu weapons. If you have any solid object around—a broom, a book, a rolled-up magazine—use the edge to jab. Don't wield it as a club.

The contents of your purse are potentially useful. A pen or comb can be used against vulnerable parts. Your keys slipped between your fingers make remarkable brass knuckles. Rings and jewelry wrapped around your fist can also be effective. If you have a spray container of perfume or breath spray, it can be used in much the same way as Mace. It must be sprayed directly in the eyes, and at closer range than Mace is used at (Mace has a range of about twelve inches), but it will have an effect. Also, your attacker won't know what you are pulling out of your purse and he may decide that you are better prepared than he thought. In a confrontation you definitely do *not* want to be wearing a necklace or pierced earrings. If your attacker were to grab them, you would find yourself at a painful disadvantage.

If the man has a weapon, you shouldn't try to fight unless absolutely necessary. If you have to fight, keep moving as fast as possible.

Dealing with a club is like dealing with any stronger person. Stay back, and, if you must, block against his arm rather than against the club.

If he has a knife, get your coat off and wrap it around your arm as

If he leans forward, grab his hair and double him over

Claw at eyes; use Mace

Blow to ear or temple

Slam heel of hand up under chin or nose

Poke to hollow of throat

Jab to solar plexus

Snap knee into groin (do not try a kick unless it is very fast)

Wrench little finger; try to break it

Kick to kneecap

If grabbed from rear, bring heel down over kneecap

Keep kicks aimed low

a shield. Try to get your belt off, and strike with the buckle end. If he grabs the belt with his free hand, let go and try to kick him when he's off balance. Whatever you do, even if you do nothing, it's going to be a very risky situation.

Don't try arguing with a man with a gun. Hundreds of years of technology went into making the gun a highly effective mode of killing, and it is too efficient a machine to tackle with your bare hands.

Presuming you follow all of our suggestions, and you go out into the world a little better able to cope, you may be wondering about the legal problems involved in thrashing a rapist. Women do seem to be concerned with the consequences of fighting back and winning. You may be open to an assault charge, true, but then who is going to believe that you jumped a six-footer just for the hell of it? You should certainly seek out a policeman and file charges before your assailant has had a chance to charge you (which really isn't to be expected). The primary reason for your doing this is that you have a better chance of winning on a battery or attempted-rape charge than on an actual rape charge. Even if charges are brought against you, there is precious little chance of your being convicted.

We have made many suggestions about ways you can prepare yourself. Remember that you aren't expected to follow all of them all of the time. You must make your own sensible decisions about how well you want to prepare yourself and what risks you want to take. If your mother comes to pick you up some bright Sunday for an afternoon at the zoo, you may want to take with you nothing more than your own common sense. If you're taking the subway at night into a dangerous neighborhood, you will probably want your flare. You know your own life style, and you should know what kind of life you want to lead. The choices are up to you.

BASIC PROCEDURE IF YOU SHOULD BE RAPED

During the rape

Stay calm.

Talk sanely, quietly, to remind him you are a human being.

If he asks you a question that you can't answer without exciting him, say something else such as calmly, factually stating, "You're hurting my arms."

Memorize the details of his face and clothing, and describe him to yourself.

Think about something concrete and routine, such as what you should do later.

Don't show any pain or weakness if you can avoid it, for it will only make him more violent.

Whether to report to the police

Can you give a clear description?

Did you know him well?

Did you do anything which could be interpreted as provocative?

How were you dressed?

Do you have bruises?

Did he use a weapon?

Did he commit any other crimes, such as theft?

Do you have the kind of background that will support an investigation?

If reported to the police

Don't take a bath.

If possible, call a friend first, then the police. If the police arrive first, wait until your friend gets there.

Don't take any flak from anybody.

Insist on going to the hospital.

Give as clear and comprehensive a description of your attacker as possible.

At the hospital

Ask for antibiotics for VD.

Consider your medical background before you accept the "morning after" pill.

Have your friend check all medication given you.

Later

Confer with your friends and local political groups about taking appropriate personal action against your attacker. There are many things that can be done, such as singling him out to the rest of the community. If you do this, first make sure you have the right man, and second, be aware of possible legal ramifications for your actions.

If you don't want to report it

Don't take a bath.

Find a friend.

Get yourself to a doctor—you may later decide to report the rape.

Get treatment for VD.

If you must go to a hospital, remember that you don't necessarily have to talk to the police.

Consider appropriate personal action.

Thursday nite
Kathleen—
I'm O.K.—everything's O.K. now. Hitching had been fine
—I was feeling very good 'cuz all my rides had been so
nice—all men (women never pick up hitchers!) with
whom I'd had good conversation as a person—I mean
no sexual overtones. Then he picked me up outside of
———, I had only 4 hrs. to go. A new red pick-up. He was
about 40, very nice and not too friendly. When he turned
off at an exit I was shocked and told him I'd get out
there. He told me no . . . I'll leave out most of his con-
versation, for the moment the ride turned into something
sexual, his pleasant conversation turned into the crudest
and most vulgar sentences I've ever listened to. He talked
that way continuously—and the words along with the
physical act humiliated me in a way the act couldn't have
by itself. He took me up a small dirt road miles into the
woods. I was shaking—but couldn't believe it was true.
When he slowed for a turn I grabbed my purse, opened
the door, and jumped—but he caught me by the wrist
and dragged me back in. He showed me a knife and told
me he didn't want to hurt me, and wouldn't, if I was nice.
I was "nice." Realizing that he would kill me—well, I
can't describe the fear. I'd never felt like that before. The
humiliation and anger I felt during the rape was nothing
in comparison. He was shocked that I'd never been
raped before—"That's" (he said) "just part of the fun of
hitchhiking." I got the feeling this wasn't a first for him
with a hitchhiker. I didn't speak or move. Afterward,
when I started to get out of the car, he told me it was a
long walk back to the highway and he would take me
'cuz he was a nice guy. He was very matter of fact after-

ward and dropped me at the highway telling me to have a nice trip.

I was lucky in many ways to have Jane, for not only did she stay with me at the hospital and the police, but she fed me, got me high (on beer), virtually tucked me in bed, and in every way was totally calm, accepting, and very nice. If her brother-in-law hadn't set up the appointment for me with the captain of homicide, I could tell I would never have been believed. After all, I was hitch-hiking and wore no bra. The captain used those words in telling me why the prosecutor would probably not prosecute 'cuz the case would never win with a jury. But he said it in such a way that he meant it was fucked up— but he'd seen it happen too many times. The pig will be picked up, tho, and held for 20 hrs. [She had taken down the man's license-plate number.] Then they'll have to release him when the prosecutor won't prosecute. I signed the no-prosecution papers which he's going to date after the pig's been held for 20 hrs. He said that the swine would be dealt with roughly—that the cops had their own ways of dealing with the law breakers they knew couldn't be prosecuted. As much as I abhor that in principle, I'm overjoyed that he might get rough treatment. The captain was speaking from outraged chivalry —but that's O.K. He spoke about how fucked up the rape laws were—how they should be changed to assault and then he could prosecute the hundreds of bastards he sees go free daily. He surprised me.

I'm in bed now and am taking the bus to ——— tomorrow morning where John will pick me up . . . I'm not hitching the rest of the trip, tho that seriously depletes my money. My first inclination was to come home. I still half want to—but I've planned this trip for so long—was so very excited about it—probably would stay in the house all the time. I can't let him do that to me, 'cuz I like the part of me that wants adventure and excitement and is undaunted to go exploring the world alone. I don't want him to kill that—just to modify it. I realize now *how much more careful I must be. And it's possible to take more precautions to insure my safety without denying myself this trip. I'm really O.K.*

All I feel in relation to him is joy in my possible vengeance—in his probable discomfort and pain. I don't know what I would have done had I not had someone to turn to. The rape wasn't so bad—it's just the idea that he had the nerve to do something like that—the gall to do it so calmly, as if he was eating breakfast—the fact that he didn't give one thought as to what conceivable right he had to use my body. It was like, if it's there, I'll take it.

Oh, he tried to offer me money afterward. I refused, not because I didn't want to stoop to taking his money, but for legal reasons. I'm sure if I took it, it would no longer be considered rape. The captain is going to call Jane to tell her the progress on the case—she wants him caught and beat up as much as I do—and I'm going to call her later. I hope it didn't hurt you for me to write in such detail. For some strange reason, your working on the rape book made me think it was O.K. to write it all to you. Also, it made me feel better to write it all down. Don't worry about me. I might have been stupid when I left Chicago, hitching against everyone's advice—but, believe me, I'll be anything but stupid about my safety now.

With much love,

CHAPTER EIGHT

Psychological Reactions

Rape victims rarely commit suicide. Rape victims rarely go insane. If they neither kill themselves nor go insane, it doesn't mean that they haven't been raped. Rape is seriously traumatizing, but it isn't a fate worse than death.

In a rape situation the woman has had her relatively secure life threatened and drastically disrupted. She's been subjected to a humiliating violation, and may have been put in real physical danger. Perhaps for the first time she's been forced to realize that such ugly things can happen to her: not to a stranger, not to her cousin, not to her friend, but to her. She will somehow have to absorb this incident and carry on in a world which will never be as secure as it once appeared to be.

Eventually the effects of a rape, like any other disaster, can be overcome, and the woman can go on, possibly as a stronger person. But it may be a long, painful recovery.

Reactions of the victim

The initial reaction usually hits as shock, anxiety, and enormous agitation. The victim may respond with crying and hysteria, but more often she may become supernaturally calm. Unfortunately, even this calm is deceptive and she probably will not be thinking or acting rationally at a time when she has to take care of several things, any one of which may be a trauma in itself, such as talking to the police or getting medical attention. She has to decide whether or not to tell anyone at all, or whom to trust. Under any circumstances these would be trying questions, and the woman isn't going to find it easy to give rational answers.

The victim who shows an outward calm is probably in a state of shock. She isn't unconcerned, just stunned. For example, the housewife who is at the Laundromat just before the attack returns to do her laundry. She thinks, Well, now what do I do? and attempts to stabilize her life by going through normal routines. Usually she gets over this and then goes into a more volatile reaction.

The first phase is finished when the woman resolves her general anxiety and returns to her normal life style. This may be a matter of days or weeks, depending on the victim and the circumstances. With most women, it happens very quickly.

The second phase is one in which the victim makes what outwardly appears to be a satisfactory adjustment. The immediately upsetting issues are settled; she's already dealt with the police and the hospital, and she's told everyone she saw fit to tell. It's time for her to carry on with her life. She's no longer acutely upset, and she tells people that things are back to normal and that she's all right now.

But the problem is usually only suppressed: she can't go on with her life if she continues to think about what has happened. Her feelings are too powerful to be dealt with. So in order to go on functioning and to reassure those concerned with her, she outwardly and inwardly denies her strongest reactions.

She may decide to continue with her life exactly as before, in an attempt to deny to herself and to others that she was violated in any way except physically. The victim may keep up deliberately dangerous habits rather than admit that the incident has affected her. Thus she rationalizes the effects of the rape. Statements come out like "It wasn't really so bad—I wasn't a virgin anyway, and he didn't really hurt me, so everything's O.K."

Any thoughts that go beyond this are set aside. It is not yet the time for her to recognize her anger against her assailant, or the anger she may be directing against herself. Throughout this time the victim may be conscious of the incident through dreams, daydreams, or occasional reminders. But since these reactions aren't as bad as the initial response, she can perceive them as insignificant.

At this time the victim has little or no desire for outside help. She may well resent it. Her emotional well-being depends on her believing that she has coped with the matter and she needs time to adjust.

Some women, however, never get out of this stage; they keep the incident repressed for years, or perhaps their entire life. It's difficult to know whether or not these women should be shaken out of phase two, or how serious it is for them to repress their reactions. No one has studied the long-range effect of rape on the victim. In any case, we strongly recommend against anyone meddling with whatever solution a woman has chosen. But there is one suggestion we can make to the woman involved. If you have been raped and think that you have adjusted, examine your life for changes in your behavior since the attack. If the changes are destructive in any way, you should probably try to confront the situation rather than ignore it.

The normal progression to phase three begins when and if the victim becomes depressed and spends a great deal of time painfully reliving the incident. As her awareness of what has happened to her increases, so does her depression, which spirals downward until she at last is forced to resolve whatever fears, angers, or guilt feelings she may have. Depression is psychologically normal for most women who have undergone a rape or severe rape attempt; it isn't a sign of weakness, or an indication that the woman is lapsing into insanity. It's a difficult time, and she may need professional help to get through it. But it's a stage to be expected.

Phase three is when the victim has to resolve her feelings about her assailant, her world, and herself. She can no longer deny that her world isn't as safe as it was before, and she has to cope with that fact. Perhaps she will limit her activities, or move to a different neighborhood, or get a dog, or change her life style in some other way. She may decide it's more important to put her energies into doing something constructive to stop rape rather than in merely altering her life style.

The woman has to re-establish her security. She must determine how this terrible thing came about, if it could happen again, and exactly how she can go on in a world that is so threatening. Of course, all this depends on the sort of person she is, her individual background, the sort of trauma she's undergone, and countless other factors.

If, for instance, she was attacked in her own house and her life was threatened, she may have a terrifying problem with security. If she was attacked by someone she knew, or with whom she had been friendly, she may have to readjust her personal dealings with people in general, and with men in particular.

The difference between a violent rape by a stranger and the more subtle rape by an acquaintance may be so great that the woman doesn't see the connection between the two. The circumstances, her endangerment, and her feelings afterward will be different. The former may cause a more violent shock to her emotions. The latter will probably bring on more confusion about her own feelings and behavior.

Phase three is also the time for the woman to resolve any negative feelings she may have about herself. If, for example, she believes that any decent woman would have fought to the death, or that she *must* have brought it on herself in some way, she may have a deep-seated problem of guilt to overcome. She may examine her every thought, gesture, or movement to see what could have implicated her in the crime. A woman who answered our questionnaire was raped by a neighbor who broke into her house at night and threatened to kill her children. She wrote: "Having searched my mind, I can honestly say that I had done absolutely nothing provocative to encourage this man or any others. My bedroom drapes are always closed and while I wear shorts while gardening they are Bermuda length as I have bad varicose veins, same reason no mini skirts."

The victim may feel guilty because she has had fantasies about rape; she may feel that somehow she must have wanted it to happen. Fantasy, of course, is far, far removed from reality. In a rape fantasy you pick the man (usually attractive) who rapes you, you direct his actions, and you pick the circumstances. In your fantasy world you are in complete control of everything, but because it is rape you're also relieved of any responsibility. It is sex without sin. Any woman who is deep into this fantasy would be snapped out of it faced with the brutal reality. Of course, there are women who have rape fantasies simply because they enjoy the whole idea of being victims of dominance and brutality; there are some very self-destructive people in the world. But this is not the ordinary woman, or the ordinary rape fantasy.

There are women who feel guilty because they became sexually aroused during the rape, or because they climaxed. Sexual feelings don't mean that the woman is necessarily implicated, or that she enjoys humiliation. One's body isn't completely coordinated with one's mind, and a woman may have a physical reaction even while, mentally, she is horrified and revolted. The excitement of terror can trigger a reaction so similar to sexual arousal that your body cannot distinguish between them. It's the same sort of misdirection as when children get excited and wet their pants. The body isn't always perfectly aligned with the mind.

Some women suffer from guilt because they feel they should have known better, or because they didn't take the obvious steps against their assailants. Using hindsight, it's always easy to determine what should have been done; it isn't so easy in a terrifying situation. It's entirely likely that the woman simply wasn't thinking that she might be raped; after all, it isn't healthy to be constantly worried about someone attacking you. Once in the situation, she may not have acted strongly because she was frightened, or because she had just never been in that sort of situation before and was completely at a loss.

She may feel guilty simply because the rape was an illicit sexual experience. If she was taught to place a high value on virginity or fidelity, she may view herself as somehow damaged. There is a great myth about the overwhelming effect of rape on a virgin. While no studies have been conducted, it seems likely that the effect depends much more on the woman's personality than on the existence or nonexistence of her hymen.

What appears to be guilt, however, may be the way the woman's mind interprets a positive impulse, a need to be in control of her life. If the woman can believe that somehow she got herself into the situation, if she can feel that in some way she caused it, if she can make herself responsible for it, then she's established a sort of control over the rape. It wasn't someone arbitrarily smashing into her life and wreaking havoc. The unpredictability of the latter situation can be too much for some women to face: if it happened entirely without provocation, then it could happen again. This is too horrifying to believe, so the victim creates an illusion of safety by declaring herself responsible for the incident. Similarly, a woman may need to deny that anyone could objectify her and negate her as a person. She instinctively realizes that the man wouldn't have raped another *person,* so she must refuse to believe that he did it to her. Declaring herself a participant gives her back her sense of self.

She can also stabilize her life by rationalizing about the rapist. If she can classify him, all she has to do is avoid that type of man to feel safe. For example, if she is a white woman who was raped by a black man, she may shun black men. Avoiding a certain type of man, or all men, can be a necessary temporary step. In most cases, the woman will eventually learn to deal with the kind of man she fears. In other cases, it's easier or more practical to learn to function without them.

The victim will somehow have to work out her feelings toward her attacker. As she begins to realize her resentment toward the man for using her in such a brutal manner, she releases the anger and directs it somewhere other than at herself. Anger can be a positive force. It can give a woman the energy, the strength, the determination to make whatever changes are necessary. For many women, anger isn't an acceptable emotion. But in this case a woman *has* to deal with it somehow. Perhaps she's the sort of person who just sits down and cries, or maybe she breaks bottles. Perhaps she writes poetry. Perhaps she just holds up her head and decides that no one is going to push her around again.

After she's resolved all the fear and anger, she'll probably feel better than she has in months, or years. This is the time for her to establish herself as a worthwhile human being who has been wronged, and who will no longer accept such treatment. She should be making constructive changes in her life. She should concentrate on recognizing unhealthy factors and changing them. If she has tolerated poor treatment by men, she should understand why she once accepted that treatment. Now she must learn to conduct her life differently.

To friends and relatives

Anyone close to a woman who has to go through all this will also have a difficult time. It's important for them to think clearly and not to let their anger get out of control. The woman needs comforting:

not rage, not revenge, not a profound economic and political explanation. Maybe someone close to her wants to go out and thrash the man, but it is better to put feelings aside and take care of her. Immediately afterward she'll need a lot of support. She should be soothed, reassured. Her immediate medical problems must be cared for; she needs a companion and a protector. She's just had an intimately upsetting experience and she needs someone to relate to her on a basic human level of warmth and protection.

While she's going through the second, seemingly calm stage, she shouldn't be forced out of it; she'll come out of it in time. She doesn't need the additional strain of your well-intended pressuring. She's just withdrawn to get a little peace.

Help should be available, but she should be left alone until she feels she's ready to talk things over. She'll have to get over it at her own speed. Then she'll need someone quiet and supportive.

Sometimes a woman may insist that the rape hasn't affected her when it's obvious that it has. While this response is to be expected during phase two, it shouldn't continue. Some women feel that they should be strong enough to absorb anything. That's a macho trip. People are overtly or subtly affected by everything that happens to them over the course of their lives, and a rape is bound to affect them. A woman has to accept it as a force to be dealt with.

To parents

It's very upsetting to have to warn children about rape. They must be taught that the world isn't as perfect a place as they think it is. That's one of the hardest parts of being a parent.

Children should be cautioned that if someone does something that they don't understand, they should go to their parents and tell them about it. No frightening or detailed description is necessary. If something happens, the parents should stay calm. If a child's been molested, it's entirely likely that she won't quite understand what happened, and she'll just be worried and upset. The extent of damage depends largely on the child and the circumstances. Certainly it will only make matters worse if she is made to feel that something horrible has happened to her and that she's changed and unclean. She should be treated as though she had been struck by someone.

In an actual rape it's likely that physical damage has occurred, and the child should be taken to a hospital. A gynecological examination will almost surely have to be made. The child should be given a general anaesthetic, so that she is not subjected to a further trauma.

Afterward she may have nightmares and other reactions, but again, no studies have been conducted and no one has a clear idea what damage may result. It depends on the individual child and the circumstances. The same advice, of course, should be given to a male child.

The same suggestions apply to a teenage child. She (or he) should trust the parents enough to come to them. If parent and child are truly alienated, there is no easy solution for that, and certainly not during a time of crisis. But a parent's opinion probably means more to a child than one may think. When a child comes to a parent and says that she's been raped, she shouldn't be treated harshly, even if she has behaved unwisely. She needs someone to trust.

Mothers should discuss sex and rape with their teenage sons. This has traditionally been left to the father, but the practice of handing down male attitudes from one generation to another perpetuates the division of emotions that causes rape. A mother has as great a responsibility to see that her son does not become a rapist as she has to see that her daughter does not become a victim.

In court everybody comes under attack, the attorneys, the judge, the victim, and the accused. It's the last blood sport with human beings trying to fight each other to death with words.
　　　　Terri Schultz, "Rape, Fear, and the Law"

Past experience has shown that many rape complaints are not legitimate. The best officer, by his efficient handling of the preliminary investigation, can do a great deal to help prove or disprove a rape complaint . . . Separating the truth from the lie is a difficult job.
　　　　Opening passage of the Chicago Police
　　　　Department Training Bulletin for
　　　　rape investigations.
　　　　Terri Schultz, "Rape, Fear, and the Law"

My morality tells me that if a girl says no, I don't try anything else. But in the black community, it's perfectly proper for a guy to walk down the street, grab a girl, and take her in an alley for a little pussy. The girls on the street at night expect it; they're looking for it too. In some areas of the black community, if she says no she just gets slapped up a little and it's all right.
　　　　A white public defender, Chicago.
　　　　Terri Schultz, "Rape, Fear, and the Law"

These women have no reason to lie. Sometimes there's a love triangle, where a woman yells "rape" to get even

*with a guy, but you can screen those cases out easily
enough. But, for God's sake, when the woman never saw
the guy before in her life, and she tells you he raped her
in the park or in the hallway, and she identifies him
. . . what more corroboration should a judge need? Why
isn't this woman's word good enough?*

> Detective Al Simon, Central Park District,
> New York Police Department.
> Martha Weiman Lear, "What Can You Say about
> Laws That Tell a Man: If You Rob a Woman,
> You May As Well Rape Her Too—
> the Rape Is Free?"

---

*I've traced the corroboration requirement back to 1860,
when I first saw it coming into the law. Why was this law
passed? Well, maybe one of our prominent senators in
those days was accused of molesting a barmaid—maybe
he actually did molest a barmaid—and he and his
learned colleagues passed this law to protect themselves
. . . this capricious law which does not apply in any
other crime.*

> Frederick J. Ludwig, Chief Assistant
> "States" Attorney, Queens.
> Martha Weiman Lear, "What Can You Say about
> Laws That Tell a Man: If You Rob a Woman,
> You May As Well Rape Her Too—
> the Rape Is Free?"

CHAPTER NINE

"I Thought the Rape Was Bad . . ."

When you get away, or the man leaves, the ordeal isn't over. You now have some decisions to make, and since you will probably not be thinking clearly enough to make them then, you ought to try to decide some things now. Are you going to report it to the police? If so, are you going to try for a conviction? That is, are you willing to go through all the legal procedures, the confrontations with the rapist, the courtroom scene? If you go to the hospital, should you take the "morning after" pill or wait to see if a pregnancy results?

You really need to know what you're going to be dealing with, what attitudes you will probably run into, and how the laws work concerning rape.

As we indicated earlier, the social mores about rape have little or no concern with protecting the woman as an individual. The official laws of this country reflect these attitudes perfectly: they treat women as property.

As we have already mentioned, a woman cannot be raped by her husband. If your husband forces you, whether by threat or actual physical injury, to have intercourse with him, you cannot have him arrested for rape. The consent question doesn't even enter into the picture. Your husband may admit that you refused. He may even admit that he used physical coercion. The right to your body belongs to him, not to you. You don't have the right to keep your husband from his property. Therefore he cannot be convicted of rape.

111

The same property concept is used in defense of an accused rapist. If it can be shown that you have ever slept with a man who is not your husband, or even that you have a "reputation" for not being chaste, your case will almost certainly be lost. A "proper" woman will belong to someone, somewhere. If she's not "proper," she's unworthy and beneath the protection of the law.

The legal concepts reflect the male concept of rape, making the law hopelessly incapable of providing real justice. Take three women: a virgin, a faithful wife, and a prostitute. The theory goes that the virgin belongs to her future husband ("I want to save myself for my husband") and is safeguarded by her father; therefore she is considered raped if forced by anyone before she is married. The faithful wife belongs to her husband; therefore she is raped if she is forced by anyone *besides* her husband. The prostitute belongs to no one; therefore she can be claimed by anyone. If a virgin is talking to an acquaintance and he forces her to have intercourse, it's rape. If a "faithful" wife is talking to someone besides her husband and he forces her, it's rape. If a prostitute is talking to an acquaintance and he forces her, it isn't rape. The same man could have attacked all three. He could have attacked them in precisely the same way. But in the eyes of the law, only the first two women were raped.

The example we used was of a prostitute; but you may well be subject to the same line of attack yourself, even if you are the most pure-hearted virgin or faithful wife. Can you *prove* yourself to be completely innocent to the D.A. and the police? The burden of proof is on you. The slightest indication of seductiveness—a short skirt, smiling when he first approached you—is taken as confirmation that you not only enjoyed the encounter but precipitated it.

Granted it *is* a problem to prove anyone's thoughts beyond a shadow of a doubt, but in the case of rape the courts have stretched this point beyond all reason. Surely no woman has consented to intercourse if the man has to hold a knife to her throat. But if she was hitchhiking, or in the man's apartment, she is going to have a hard time proving that she was raped. In the interests of protecting the man, the courts will overlook the matter of the knife.

Of course, the progress of justice is further determined by level of income, by race, and by occupation, as well as by social reputation. Where a poor black woman would be ignored, a rich white one could probably get a conviction. But don't begrudge the rich their influence. It's rare enough that any women get justice.

The reason the whole procedure is so difficult is that you will have to deal entirely with a man's world, where you will be subject to the same attitudes men display elsewhere. Some of these men may be sympathetic, depending on the individuals you encounter and the brutality of the rape. But you'll still be dealing with policemen, male doctors, male interns, male lawyers, and male judges. Men are in the positions of power. And inasmuch as our society promotes and perpetuates certain types of rape, you can't expect to turn to the bastions of that same society for protection.

The police are unable and, to some extent, unwilling to make arrests in most of the cases reported to them. Of the men actually charged with rape, a very small minority are convicted. One of the few studies we found on the subject set the figure at less than one-tenth. When you consider that the FBI estimates that only one-sixth of all *legal* rapes are reported, that a fraction of these result in arrests, and that about one-tenth of the arrested end in convictions, you begin to see how inadequately women are protected by the law. Try to keep all that in mind when you are deciding whether, and how, to deal with the legal system.

If you decide to go to the police, here are some things you can do so that you will be taken seriously. First, report the rape to the first people you encounter, with one exception: don't tell it to a strange man who is alone. There are cases recorded of double rapes, in which the man who was asked for help raped the woman himself. If the people you report it to are respectable, they can be valuable witnesses.

Most states accept the testimony of persons who will state that the victim told them about the rape immediately after the occurrence and that she appeared to be upset. Witnesses are an important verification of your story. If these people are willing to go with you to the police station, it may be more likely that you will be believed.

If you don't see anyone, call a friend. Pick a very good friend, because you will probably be spending the next few hours together, and it will be very hard on her too. Then call the police at once. The sooner the rape is reported, the more likely it is that there will be an arrest. (If you call the police first, insist that they wait until your friend arrives before they take you to the hospital, unless, of course, you are seriously injured.)

When the police come, they will take you and your friend to the nearest hospital that handles rape cases. Not all hospitals do; in Chicago we found that not even *most* hospitals do. Their reasons vary. Many Catholic hospitals refuse rape cases because proper treatment would include some measure toward preventing pregnancy. Apparently they believe that even a conception resulting from rape is God's will. Private hospitals often turn away rape victims because they want to avoid legal entanglements, i.e., having doctors presenting evidence in court. One of the reasons given is that, legally, special techniques are required to establish the presence of sperm in the woman. As far as we've been able to determine, all that is required is that a smear be taken, examined, and turned over to the investigating office. In any case, for these and other reasons, there may be surprisingly few hospitals to which the police can take you.

There are two important reasons for going to a hospital. First, the doctors can prevent pregnancy. Second, they can help establish proof of intercourse. They can also treat you for any physical injuries you may have received during the rape—perhaps torn tissue, if the man was particularly violent. This is rare, but if you're feeling internal pain, you should certainly see a doctor.

Once you get to the hospital, there will be only so much that they can do for you. No matter how bad you feel, the emergency room will take care only of your immediately pressing physical problems. That is their purpose. They will do what they can to help you physically. In more extreme cases, they may go so far as to administer tranquilizers to sustain you until you can find more comprehensive care.

In the emergency room, you will have to tell the attendant that you were raped. You will be given a form to sign, giving your consent to treatment. If it is going to be painful emotionally to talk about what happened, you don't have to tell the hospital workers any extraneous details of the attack. If the doctor asks an embarrassing question, don't be afraid to ask why he or she needs to know.

You will have to undergo an examination by a gynecologist. In an examining room you will partially undress, lie down on a table, and be covered with a sheet. When the gynecologist comes, you will put your heels into a pair of stirrups at the end of the table so that your legs are spread and your genitals are accessible. This is standard procedure for any vaginal examination, and for those of you who go to a gynecologist regularly, it may seem unnecessary to explain it in detail. But not every woman who gets raped has had experience with this sort of examination, and under the best of conditions the first time can be frightening. Rape is not the best of circumstances.

The gynecologist will examine you with the aid of a speculum, a duck-billed sort of instrument. He or she will insert the speculum into your vagina and open it so that your cervix and vaginal tract can be seen, to check for sperm or any other signs of recent intercourse, such as a torn hymen. The doctor will take a smear and then remove the speculum and examine you for any other injuries.

The examination is uncomfortable even if it is carefully done. If it is done with brutal efficiency, it may be quite painful. If that happens, remember the doctor's name and report him or her to the administration later. It won't help you, but there is the possibility that the doctor will have to be more gentle with other women in the future. You may prefer to have your own doctor perform the examination.

After it has been established that you have had recent intercourse, the doctors will try to determine whether you are likely to become pregnant. They will ask if you are using any method of birth control, such as the pill or an IUD. They will ask the dates of your last few periods to determine whether you may be fertile. If there is any possibility that you may become pregnant, you may be given a massive dose of diethylstilbestrol, a synthetic substance related to estrogen and known as DES, or the "morning after" pill. If you have to take the pill, you will probably get sick.

This enormous dose is designed to temporarily disrupt your hormonal balance, and will probably wreak havoc on your system. Among the possible side effects are nausea and vomiting, abdominal pain and distress, swelling and tenderness of the breasts, a chronic lack of appetite, diarrhea, weariness, tingling sensations, dizziness, headaches, anxiety, the appearance of purple blotches on the skin, and various allergic reactions. The drug may also aggravate conditions of epilepsy, migraine, asthma, and cardiac or renal dysfunction. In addition, there appear to be some links between this drug and vaginal cancer. We don't mean to suggest that all of this will occur if you take the drug. But we have talked to perfectly healthy young women who experienced many or most of the side effects. Your system will correct itself fairly soon. Meanwhile, you may be a very sick woman. You may also have the scare of your life when your period fails to appear at the proper time, especially if your doctor fails to inform you that that is a common side effect.

DES is effective only if administered within twenty-four hours after intercourse. You may want to ask for a "D and C" instead (dilation and curettage), which is now a legal procedure. This is how most abortions are performed. If done soon after intercourse, it isn't considered an abortion, as it takes some time for the sperm to meet the ovum and for the ovum to implant itself in the wall of the uterus. However, the hospital may not want to do it.

You may prefer to take the chance that you won't get pregnant, intending to take action if you do. There is a new procedure called menstrual extraction, which can be performed if your period fails to appear. Menstrual extraction is the removal of the uterine lining by suction through a very narrow tube inserted through the cervix. In many cases, the tube, or cannula, can be inserted without anaesthetizing the patient or dilating the cervix. It is considered by many to be far superior to a D and C because it is faster, less complicated, and there is less risk of uterine perforation. It must be performed within five to ten days after the date menstruation is due, and you needn't have a pregnancy test beforehand. As the incidence of pregnancy from random intercourse is only 5 percent, you may choose to put off a decision about this problem until later, that is, until your period is due. There is certainly no need to put yourself through any more than is necessary. Extraction now makes this an acceptable alternative.

Have your friend keep track of any medication you are given. You may receive pain killers or other medicines that can produce side effects. You or your friend should ask to be sure.

After about two weeks you should be checked for venereal disease since there is now a gonorrhea epidemic in this country. You can have a venereal disease with no obvious symptoms for a long, long time, but the final damage can be extensive, often fatal.

Even if you decide not to report the rape, you may want to go to a hospital. It's best to avoid large urban hospitals, or hospitals that primarily treat poor or black people. It's there that you're likely to receive the most abusive treatment. The hospital will report the rape whether you want them to or not. You will probably have to deal with the police, but you don't have to cooperate with them. Your own doctor may stretch medical duty a bit and not report it. It is a good idea to get medical attention somewhere as soon as possible. For one thing, you may change your mind about reporting the rape, and if you do, it will be too late to get medical evidence. And there is always the problem of pregnancy.

As soon as the police are contacted, they will begin questioning you to get a clear description of the man. Try to cooperate—the attacker may still be in the vicinity. If the police have a detailed description immediately after the rape, they may be able to find him. It is unlikely that they will be able to find him after he has had a chance to blend into the landscape. You will be asked for height, build, coloring, dress, any distinguishing characteristics. If you are lucid enough to think while you are being raped, these are good things to think about. That may sound callous or flippant, but you will probably be thinking of something while it is happening, and thinking of how to escape and how to describe your attacker are both better than thinking about how horrible it is and how humiliated and terrified you're feeling. If the man is in a car, try for the license number, but at least get a description. Write down the license number as soon as you can, even if that means scratching it in the dirt or writing it on the sidewalk.

After giving a description of your attacker, you will be asked to give the details of the attack. This is where your friend will be important. If you can, you should talk to your friend before the police arrive. Get all the facts straight and in their proper order, so that you don't get confused when the police start questioning you. You should try to cooperate with the police, but if it is too painful for you to talk about just then, there's no absolute necessity for them to know all the details immediately. The description is the only thing that is urgent.

Even if you are capable of talking about it, there are some questions which they have no need and no right to ask. Many women have reported to us that they were questioned by police officers who appeared to be getting voyeuristic kicks by demanding graphic answers to questions which were basically irrelevant to the investigation. There are many questions which are quite personal but are also legitimate. It is relevant for the police to ask if the rapist had an orgasm. If he did, there will be evidence of semen in the vaginal tract. If he did not, there may not be. It is nothing short of outrageous for anyone to ask if you had an orgasm. Your friend should be able to help you here by asking what the purpose of the question is. You may be in no shape to distinguish between a legitimate question and an illegitimate one. She should be able to work out what is exploitation. And you won't feel terrifyingly alone if you run into disbelief and suspicion on the part of the police.

You're likely to run into just that. If you are unmarried, if you look like a hippie or are black, if you were on the streets after dark, if it happened in your own home or his home, if you were dressed provocatively, or are ugly—any of these or a hundred other things is enough to make a policeman refuse to believe you. Either you were asking for it, or you are simply a hysterical female and it didn't happen at all. So the people to whom you turn for help may well be hostile, contemptuous, or even amused. Having a friend with you who believes you and sympathizes with you can be very important.

Remember that the police have no right to intimidate you into answering questions or doing anything else that you don't want to do. You are the victim. They may forget that, but you shouldn't. You have done nothing wrong. You should not be harassed. You and the police are supposed to be working together to apprehend a criminal and see that justice is done, even if it doesn't always feel like that. At the very worst, the police can refuse to prosecute your case. And if they are giving you a hard time, they probably aren't taking you seriously anyway.

Don't worry about restraining yourself or controlling your emotions. You have too much to worry about without that, and it may hurt you to do so. The police and the courts expect you to be distraught. No woman, according to the myths of our society, could actually go through a rape without coming close to insanity. It is, after all, a fate worse than death. If you seem calm, you are unlikely to be believed, whatever that calmness may cost you in emotional energy. Your attitude will be brought up in court as evidence. Women have been known to lose rape cases because the shock following the attack brought on a false calmness and lucidity. The police will treat you with greater care and will take your case more seriously if you allow your emotions to show.

The last paragraph was distasteful to write. Many women hate the idea of pandering to any man's preconceived notion of how a woman should behave. But the whole situation is considerably worse than distasteful. We aren't suggesting that you fake the upset, just don't fight it.

If the police do not believe your story, they may refuse to get involved. You can demand that they at least take you to a hospital; this is your right as a citizen. Beyond that, you can take further legal action without the police. If you know the man, you can walk up to him and place him under citizen's arrest, then call the police to have him brought in. The legal process will continue from there, with only one difference: if he could somehow prove that there was no basis for your charge, you would be liable for false arrest.

You have yet another option for getting him arrested. If the police refuse to become involved because, for example, your attacker had some relationship to you, you can go to the headquarters of the police district in which the crime occurred, go before the district magistrate, and swear out a complaint. If the magistrate believes you, he will issue a warrant for the man's arrest. This is the usual procedure in family fights. Again, there is the problem of a countersuit.

If you can get the man arrested, you will have done better than most women who are raped. In fact, you can consider it a real triumph. The arrest itself will be a very bad experience for him, especially if they lock him in a large urban jail. It will also be put on his record, and will make an arrest easier if he ever tries to rape another woman. But the cell, and his cellmates, his wife and his boss may just make his life miserable enough for him to lose interest. It isn't an eye for an eye, but it can be enough to convince him that all women aren't easy victims.

After the arrest, the prosecutor will take over. He may decide not to prosecute. Even if he does, it is highly likely that he'll try to make a deal with the rapist or his lawyer. The prosecutor will probably offer to drop the rape charge if the man will plead guilty to some lesser charge. If he doesn't have a very good case, the attacker will accept the deal and you won't have to go to court. Whatever happens, you have no voice in the bargaining. There are some who feel that you should try to prevent this sort of deal, but you really don't have any choice in the matter.

If the rapist's lawyer feels, however, that he has a fairly good chance of winning the case, he will probably take it to trial. This will mean you have another decision to make. We explained earlier how the rape laws work and how they reflect social patterns. The attitudes of the police are an example of this. The trial itself can far surpass anything else for sheer brutality. Many policemen have stated that they would not want their own wives or daughters to submit to a rape trial.

This isn't really surprising. It's in the logic of the law. If it can be proved that this particular man had intercourse with you (and that is usually the most that you can prove definitely), his lawyer must try to make the jury believe that you consented to it. The horror lies in *how* the lawyer goes about doing this. You will be questioned in detail about your sexual behavior, your relationship with men. If you admit to one instance of intercourse with a man not your husband, or any previous sexual contact with your attacker, your case will be lost. There are two ways of interpreting this. Either your previous straying makes the rape unimportant, or your having consented to sleep with one man who didn't legally possess you means that you would consent to any man. Either interpretation is insulting in the extreme.

The lawyer may not even have to question your purity to that extent. Testimony by one of your neighbors that you have a "bad" reputation, or that he or she has seen men leave or enter your home late at night, would probably be enough to destroy your claim of rape. The slightest suspicion, in fact, will convince a jury that "she had it coming," or that it wasn't really rape. One case was reported to us in which the victim was an ex-nun, only a few months out of the convent and still a virgin. Her house was burglarized and she was attacked. It was implied in the courtroom that this woman's leaving the convent was evidence of repressed sexual desires. The men were convicted as burglars, but acquitted of any rape charges.

Having every part of your daily life laid bare for the court, and having every past action, no matter how innocent, interpreted as evidence of promiscuity, is a miserable, frustrating experience. But your ordeal will not stop there. You will be asked to repeat in graphic detail the circumstances of the rape. On the witness stand, you cannot refuse to answer questions. You will have to deal with implications that you seduced your attacker into raping you and "loved every minute of it." If you were provocatively attired, if you responded to his advances with anything which could be interpreted as encourage-ment (if for example you answered when he said "hello"), if you said anything which might arouse him (a woman who responded with "Fuck off" when approached lost her case because "fuck" is a sexually exciting word), if it can be shown that you were guilty of any of these or a dozen other similar things, you may lose your case. It's assumed that anything that may be interpreted as misconduct on the part of the woman assures the court that she was asking for it. And no man is to be held accountable for following through. If you kiss a man at the door, and he pushes you inside and rapes you, you will probably never get the case to court, and if you do, you don't have a prayer.

Obviously you need a very good case to make going to court worthwhile. Even if you have a good case, you may not want to. There are those who argue that it is your duty to prosecute if you can. We believe that it takes a brave woman to follow a rape charge to the end. In our society, prosecuting a rapist is an act of courage. A woman who will do it is to be admired. But a woman who will not do it shouldn't be regarded with contempt.

The reasoning behind this corruption of justice is that men must be protected from unjust accusations of rape. (Somehow it seems that men need protection from accusations much more than women need protection from rape.) The idea is that if the laws regarding admis-sible evidence in rape cases were changed, there would be wholesale prosecution of innocent men by hysterical, vindictive women. As a result, rape laws are designed to protect men rather than women.

One suggestion is that the rape laws be done away with entirely, and that women be allowed to prosecute their attackers for assault. Since assault carries less emotional import, the possibility of false accusation would be lessened, it would be easier to get a conviction, and the trials would not be the brutal circuses they are now.

Also, as we explained earlier, rape laws are basically property laws. Evidence of penetration is required because only penetration is seen as a robbery of the right to sexual access. If a man attacks a woman and forces her to perform any other sexual act, it is not rape.

This view of sexuality and of the value of women is insulting and degrading. In fact, the violation lies in the attack on our selves, not our hymens or our otherwise untouched vaginas. We would like to see a law in which an attack upon a woman, any attack, would be treated seriously and with the rage which is now reserved for documented cases of forcible penetration of a "pure woman."

Some men tell us we must be patient and persuasive; that we must be womanly. My friends, what is a man's idea of womanliness? It is to have a manner which pleases him— quiet, deferential, submissive, approaching him as a subject does a master. He wants no self-assertion on our part, no defiance, no vehement arraignment of him as a robber and a criminal . . . while every right achieved by the oppressed has been wrung from tyrants by force; while the darkest page on human history is the outrages on women—shall men still tell us to be patient, persuasive, womanly?

Elizabeth Cady Stanton, in 1870

CHAPTER TEN

The Movement Against Rape

In the spring of 1972, a group of fifty or sixty women gathered in a room at the Loop YWCA in Chicago. Young and old; black, white, and brown; they were there to talk about rape. Out of that conference came the Chicago Northside Rape Crisis Line, a continuing series of self-defense classes, this book, and a group called Chicago Women Against Rape. Later, another crisis line called the Southside Rape Action Coalition was formed. None of these groups was unique. At the same time, or earlier, groups of women were getting together all over the country, preparing to fight against rape. And, though they were not connected to each other, many of these groups were taking the name WAR, Women Against Rape.

The basic principle around which all of these groups were organizing was enunciated in the first widely read statement of the anti-rape movement, "Rape: The All-American Crime," by Susan Griffin. That principle was simply this: that rape is not the isolated act of an aberrant individual but a crime against women that is encouraged by a sexist society; that women are seen, in our culture, not as whole human beings, but as objects and authorized victims of male aggression. This is the case we have tried to make in this book. It is a strong accusation, and we have stated it here in strong terms, but it is the only explanation for the incredibly high, and constantly increasing, numbers of reported rapes, and for the ways in which victims are treated by the police, courts, hospitals, and other established institutions. Women across the country have decided that the situation can no longer be tolerated.

The fight against rape is being waged in Washington, Philadelphia, St. Louis, Chicago, Detroit, San Francisco, Los Angeles. It is being carried on in large cities and small towns in the East, the Midwest, the South, and the West. Women are moving, and in some cases, they are forcing the established institutions to move. Rape squads have been established in several major police departments and changes in the corroboration requirements are being sought in many state legislatures. We cannot begin, in this one chapter, to relate all the struggles that have taken place and are taking place right now, but we can give a general idea of how the fight is going. We can, drawing from the experiences of the many groups of women who are working, make some suggestions to you and the women around you if you want to join the fight.

Many different ways of fighting have been tried in the last two or three years, and many things have been learned. At one point, in Detroit, a group of women trained in self-defense patrolled dangerous neighborhoods. There was never any way of determining whether they had any effect. They did not, in fact, find themselves rescuing women. On the other hand, their presence may have discouraged some attacks. In the end, however, the women decided that this approach was not a very practical one in terms of the time and emotional energy expended. Many of the same women were involved in putting together the handbook *Stop Rape*. This excellent pamphlet was distributed to women around the country and inspired anti-rape activities in many communities.

Street patrols were also tried on the West Coast, answering calls for help from women and trying to apprehend rapists whom the police had not arrested. Eventually, these patrols, in most places where they were tried, were abandoned for other activities. Time will tell whether or not the frustrations of dealing with the established authorities will force women once more into the streets, this time with more effective strategies.

GROUP PROJECTS

A rape crisis telephone line is often the first project of an anti-rape group, for many reasons. It offers the possibility for immediate, though often minimal, change in the situation of the woman who is raped. Inspired by the other sorts of crisis intervention activities set up for dealing with drug emergencies or suicides, for example, the crisis center has grown into one of the most significant forms of action that the women's movement has so far developed. It not only provides desperately needed support for the victim, it can also reach a woman at a moment of profound rage and help her to channel it, perhaps for the first time, outward, toward the society which caused it. Finally, because it is a concrete activity which people can understand, the rape crisis center can focus public attention on the problem of rape.

Like the other emergency lines, the rape crisis line consists of telephones staffed by people, in this case women, who are trained to give advice and help. The women on the line are prepared to explain what a rape victim must expect if she goes to the police and can help her decide if that is what she wants to do. Staff members may go with her to the police and the hospital. If she decides to prosecute, they can give her counseling and encouragement throughout the legal procedure. Or they may simply talk to the woman and help her deal with the rape in her mind and life. In some cases, they may refer her to a psychologist.

We have given, here, a general idea of how a rape crisis center operates. (For a further discussion, see the appendix.) If you are interested in forming such a group, you can write to the Washington, D.C., Rape Crisis Center, P.O. Box 21005, Kalorama Street Station, Washington, D.C. 20009, for a copy of *How to Start a Rape Crisis Center* ($1.50 a copy plus 20 cents postage). Or you might want to contact one of the centers listed in the appendix. If there is one near you, you could probably learn more on a weekend visit there than from any number of books and pamphlets.

Of course, the crisis line is not the only possible activity for an anti-rape group. It is only one front of the war. There are many others. A project that often grows out of a crisis center is a kind of legal advocacy program. After helping a woman past the police and hospitals, the crisis lines are faced with the problem of court proceedings which may continue for months or, in some cases, years. They find prosecutors who are unwilling to prosecute and male-dominated courtrooms in which the woman who is the complainant finds no support and encouragement. They soon find that dealing with the courts is a full-time project.

In Chicago, women from all of the groups working against rape got together with a feminist attorney who had been involved in giving legal counsel to rape victims. This attorney had formed rap groups of women who were going through rape trials so that they could give each other encouragement and support.

The group which was thus formed began attacking the legal situation in two ways. They trained themselves to give counsel to the victim before she goes into court, and they help the D.A. prepare the case.

At the same time, this group formulated a set of demands which they presented to the state attorney's office. They asked for improvements in the procedure. Out of this confrontation came an official liaison between the state attorney and the anti-rape groups. In Chicago, most rape cases are now prosecuted by women assistant state attorneys. Women lay advocates are allowed to be present at all pre-trial interviews as well as during the trial.

The situation as regards reforms in laws and court procedures is changing so rapidly we felt we couldn't go into it in detail. But the successes and failures in this area are a good indication of where we need to concentrate our efforts. If you are interested in this part of the fight against rape, contact the Washington, D.C., Rape Crisis Center or Chicago Legal Action for Women, c/o Loop YWCA, 37 South Wabash, Chicago, Illinois 60603.

Other approaches to the problem are possible. A tactic that originated with a black, male-run radio station in Chicago (WVON) is the receiving and broadcasting of descriptions of rapists throughout the community. In response, black policemen volunteered to investigate these cases in their off-duty hours. This idea seems to have caught on; there are at least two more black stations (in Kansas City and Louisville) that have instituted the program, which is a part of Operation Crime-Stop.

SELF-DEFENSE COURSES

The actions which we have so far described have been directed toward better treatment of the rape victim after she has been raped. The other, more important, aspect of the fight is to work toward seeing that women don't get raped. This could be a very long struggle, and until it is won, we must try to improve the situation of the woman who has been raped.

Decreasing the rape rate will require two things: that women learn to defend themselves, and that the attitudes of this society and the men in it toward women be changed. A project that concentrates on the first of these is crucial for a community of women who are trying to stop rape.

A self-defense course can be started with one good teacher and a large room. The second may be difficult to find, the first almost impossible. The ideal teacher is a woman with a good knowledge of both street fighting and karate, and a strong consciousness of the particular problems of women learning to fight after years of conditioning against violence.

The results of good self-defense courses justify the efforts necessary to set them up. Nothing compares with being able to take care of yourself.

A more ambitious project along the same lines is arranging a self-defense course in the public schools, where students will learn what they need to know before they have to use it. The problem here is that you cannot just demand that it be taught. You must be ready to suggest a teacher and stir up support from the women in the schools. No one can force a woman to learn to defend herself, but if the course is available, there will at least be an opportunity to learn for those who are interested. If you are a high-school student, you must not only convince other students in the school to join you, you must find a way to make your voice heard by adults who are accustomed to ignoring you and who will view your desire for self-reliance as a fad.

RAPE CONFERENCES

An excellent way to start community-wide interest in the problem of rape is to hold a conference, inviting women from as wide a spectrum as possible. It should be limited to women for the simple reason that the presence of men seriously inhibits free discussion of rape. A conference of this kind can bring together the women in your area who are concerned and who want to fight rape. It can also be a great consciousness-raising opportunity for other women.

Finally, women must realize that most of these projects, as important as they are, do nothing more than bandage the wounds of a sick society. The problem of rape is not a separate and distinct issue. It cannot be dealt with apart from the entire question of the position of women in this society. Women can reform laws, regulate police and hospital treatment, train themselves, and yet, so long as women are treated as less than human beings, they will be raped. Rape is only a symptom of the massive sickness called sexism, and the sickness itself must be cured.

So while I do not pray for anybody or any party to commit outrages, still I do pray, and that earnestly and constantly, for some terrific shock to startle the women of this nation into a self-respect which will compel them to see the abject degradation of their present position; which will force them to break their yoke of bondage, and give them faith in themselves; which will make them proclaim their allegiance to women first; which will enable them to see that man can no more feel, speak or act for woman than could the old slaveholder for his slave. The fact is, women are in chains, and their servitude is all the more debasing because they do not realize it. O, to compel them to see and feel, and to give them the courage and conscience to speak and act for their own freedom, though they face the scorn and contempt of all the world for doing it.

Susan B. Anthony, from a letter to a friend, summer 1870

Appendix

Questionnaires on rape were published in several underground papers and distributed at various rape conferences. All victims of rape or serious rape attempts were asked to provide certain information concerning their experiences. The respondents supplied such data as their physical characteristics, occupations, and marital status and those of their attacker or attackers, plus certain information concerning the actual attack situation itself—location, time, and whether other people were present.

The respondent was also asked if she was led into a dangerous situation, what her relationship was to the attacker, what the attitude of the attacker was, what force was utilized by the rapist, and whether or not she resisted, and if so, how she resisted. Data were obtained on whether or not the rape or rape attempt was reported to the police, what the reaction of the police was, and whether an arrest or conviction resulted. Victims were also asked to describe how the attack affected their lives, and who or what helped them to deal with the rape afterward. (The results of the questionnaire can be found in this appendix.)

Statistics on rape are difficult, if not almost impossible, to obtain. Few studies have been done on rape. This goes along with the fact that very little research has been done on women at all and rape is a crime against women. The authors had almost no past research to tap for clues as to how to conduct their study. In addition, there was a problem in distributing the rape questionnaires. Most of our respondents were readers of the student or movement newspapers that agreed to run our questionnaire or were participants at rape conferences. Thus, our sampling tended to be more white and middle-class than the norm. While it is not a representa-

133

tive group, the results are being given in the hope that they will provide some insight, guidance, and motivation for future research into this, up until now, almost totally unexplored area of crime.

The victims of our survey ranged in age from seven to thirty-nine years of age, the majority being from fifteen to twenty-one years old. Ninety-five percent of the victims were white (probably because of our sampling), and 88 percent were single at the time of the attack. Fifty-seven percent were students. There was a normal distribution according to height and weight. Thirty-eight percent of the rapists were single, 18 percent married, 11 percent widowed, separated, or divorced, and in 33 percent of the cases the marital status was unknown. Occupations differed considerably —from the rapist being the president of a business or a college lecturer to a peddler or an unemployed "deadbeat." Eighteen percent were students —this percentage was probably due to the biased nature of our sample. We could find no information to indicate that either the victims or the attackers belonged to a unique group of individuals. From all data available, it appears that "normal" men rape "normal" women.

In 43 percent of the incidents, the victim did not know the attacker at all, or only by sight. Thirty-seven percent of the rapes were initiated by men rated as acquaintances. Nineteen percent of the acquaintances were found to fit in a special category we termed "relatives or friends of close friends or relatives." Many of the victims fell into the trap of trusting a boy friend's friend, for example. The remaining 20 percent of the attacks were perpetrated by dates, friends, ex-lovers, and one by a father.

A whopping 47 percent of the rapes occurred in either the victim's or rapist's home. Staying at home doesn't necessarily mean your virtue will be kept intact. Ten percent occurred inside buildings other than the victim's or rapist's home—for example, in a friend's home or a deserted college building. Eighteen percent occurred in cars. The feedback we received on this question is what has prompted our frequent warning "Hitchhikers beware!" The remaining 25 percent of the attacks were committed in streets, alleys, parks, and in the country. (Some hitchhikers were taken to deserted areas in the country—one to the desert—and raped.)

It seems that the presence of other people can be a deterrent, but not always. In 65 percent of the cases, no other person was present at the time of the attack (except, in gang rapes, the other attackers). However, 35 percent of the victims were raped in the actual presence of others, or in situations where others were within close range. (Several said they were too embarrassed to scream. Blush if you must, but scream! Victims of rape attacks indicate that determined resistance in any form pays off. Rapists don't want an adversary or an audience.)

Time appears to be an important factor in rape occurrences. Sixty-nine percent of the attacks took place between 6 p.m. and 2:59 a.m. Rapes start slowing down at 3 a.m., hit a low (0 percent) between 6 a.m. and 8:59 a.m., and start picking up at noon, until they reach their peak between 9 p.m. and 11:59 p.m. Only one rape occurred between 6 a.m. and 11:59 a.m. (Obviously rapists aren't early risers.) Actually this statistic is not surprising, since most crimes occur under the cover of night.

Forty-three percent of the victims were aware that they were being led into a dangerous situation, 30 percent were unaware (many because they were trusting people they did not know well), and 17 percent were not in control of the situation.

The types of force used by 73 percent of the rapists included 38 percent threats, 23 percent blows, 23 percent weapons, 20 percent beatings, and 7 percent attempted chokings. (In some cases, more than one type of force was applied.) Eighty-two percent of the victims tried to resist the attack in some form. Of these, 82 percent resisted in a physical way (punching, scratching, biting, etc.), 23 percent tried to dissuade their attackers verbally, and 14 percent screamed. This study, of course, reflects only those who were unsuccessful in fighting off rape attacks. The next study that should be done would be one that indicates in what ways women have been successful in protecting and defending themselves.

The attitudes of the rapists proved enlightening. They certainly didn't seem to be "animals desperate for sexual release." In 42 percent of the cases, the victims described the attacker's attitude as matter-of-fact or calm. (Many of these attitudes appeared in combinations.) Sixty percent of the rapists were said to be hostile or contemptuous, or both; 22 percent were described as angry, 22 percent as righteous, and 13 percent as frightened. Of course, the way our legal system is set up, the rapist doesn't have much to fear.

Seventy percent of the victims did not report the crime. Of the cases in which the rape was reported, 33 percent of the rapists were apprehended. Out of the rapists who were caught, 50 percent were convicted. This was a grand total of three convictions out of sixty rapes! In only *one* case were the rapists convicted on the charge of rape. (This was a situation where three men forced entrance into a couple's home and raped the woman in the presence of her husband.) In another incident, the rapist was convicted of assault. In the third instance, *both* the rapist and the victim were convicted. Unfortunately, this respondent did not explain the circumstances in any detail. (One case is still pending.) Of the five victims who went to court, only two felt that they received fair treatment.

In many cases the first people the victim sees after the rape are the police. Forty-four percent of those who reported the rape described the

Attitude of Attacker	Not at All $T = 20$	By Sight $T = 6$	FAMILIARITY Acquaintance $T = 22$
Hostile	45%	67%	18%
Contemptuous	35%	17%	27%
Angry	10%	33%	27%
Frightened	0%	17%	18%
Matter-of-fact	35%	33%	41%
Righteous	20%	0%	27%

police as unsympathetic or downright intimidating. Thirty-eight percent said they were helpful, and 18 percent did not answer the question.

After studying the questionnaires, we concluded that many of the victims were affected in similar ways by the attack. From this information, various categories were formed and the way or ways that each respondent was affected was recorded. The results are as follows: 42 percent reported feeling afraid of men, 28 percent said it affected their lives sexually, 27 percent related that it made them feel less independent or more afraid of being on their own, 23 percent said it damaged their trust in male-female relationships, 18 percent reported feelings of worthlessness or loss of self-respect, 17 percent felt hostile toward men, 10 percent sustained physical injuries, 7 percent reported suicidal impulses as a result, and 5 percent reported having nightmares following the incident.

Fifty percent of the victims said that no one helped them to deal with the rape's psychological effects. Of those who received some assistance, 25 percent talked it out with friends. Feminist or women's groups helped 12 percent, professional counseling was sought by 8 percent, 3 percent received some support from a relative, and 2 percent (or one victim) received psychological support at the hospital.

While analyzing the various rape accounts, it was noted that certain variables appeared to be linked in a large number of cases. The victim's relationship to the attacker, the attacker's attitude, the amount of violence used in the rape, and the location of the crime seemed interrelated.

First, let us consider the woman's relationship to the rapist and his attitude.

Friend $T = 2$	*Date* $T = 7$	*Ex-Lover* $T = 2$	*Relative* $T = 1$
0%	14%	50%	0%
0%	29%	50%	100%
50%	29%	0%	0%
50%	29%	0%	0%
50%	71%	50%	0%
0%	0%	50%	100%

Note that as the level of familiarity increases, the percentage of rapists described as hostile tends to decrease and the percentage described as matter-of-fact or calm tends to increase. (These percentages do not add up to 100 percent because the rapist was described as having more than one characteristic in some instances. The data for friend, ex-lover, and relative are based on such a small sample that they can hardly be considered conclusive.)

Next let us examine the relationship between the woman's degree of familiarity with the rapist and the violence of the attack. A violent rape has been defined for the purpose of comparison as one that involved a weapon, beating, or choking, or any combination of the three. A non-violent rape is one where the force consisted of hitting, overpowering, or threat, or any combination of these. We found that hitting and beating did not necessarily go hand in hand. This is why hitting was not included as part of a violent rape. A rapist who beats women and a rapist who merely hits her may be very different types of people.

An attempt was also made to find a possible relationship between the number of people present and the use of different types of force. No relationship could be discovered except in the category of hitting. In 86 percent of the cases where hitting occurred, no other person was present. It seems that hitting a victim (but not beating) may be a somewhat personal matter to a rapist. (At least something is personal to them . . .)

RAPES AND ATTEMPTED RAPE—FAMILIARITY WITH ATTACKER

VIOLENCE OF RAPE	Not at All	By Sight	Acquaintance	Date
Violent	60%	67%	23%	29%
Non-violent	40%	33%	77%	71%

(The categories of friend, ex-lover, and relative have been disregarded when observing these trends because of an inadequate number of cases.)

If serious rape attempts are removed from this sample and we consider only completed rapes, the trend is even more significant.

COMPLETED RAPES—FAMILIARITY WITH ATTACKER

VIOLENCE OF RAPE	Not at All	By Sight	Acquaintance	Date
Violent	75%	60%	24%	20%
Non-violent	25%	40%	76%	80%

Thus, in completed rapes, the degree of familiarity is inversely proportional to the violence of the attack.

There also appears to be a relationship between hostile, contemptuous attackers and the degree of violence utilized in a rape.

VIOLENCE OF RAPE	ATTITUDE OF RAPIST					
	Hostile	Contemptuous	Angry	Frightened	Matter-of-fact	Righteous
Violent	48%	50%	20%	16%	32%	28%
Non-violent	20%	11%	23%	11%	49%	14%

Thus the most violent rapes tend to be committed by hostile or contemptuous rapists, and chances of encountering a hostile, contemptuous rapist are highest when you don't know him at all.

The location of the attack and the amount of violence used also suggest a pattern. The most violent rapes tend to be committed in alleys, streets, and the country. The least violent take place in the rapist's home. This is presented in the following table:

LOCATION OF ATTACK

VIOLENCE OF RAPE	Country	Alley	Street	Car	Own Home	Park	Indoors	Rapist's Home
Violent	75%	67%	60%	45%	36%	33%	33%	29%
Non-violent	25%	33%	40%	55%	67%	67%	67%	71%

(These statistics certainly do not mean to imply that a woman is safe in a rapist's home, however. The majority of rapes are still committed in the rapist's or victim's home. They mean that if the rape takes place in his home there is less chance that it will be a rape involving a weapon, beating, or choking.) The location of the rape also relates to how well the victim is acquainted with the rapist.

SPECIFIC RESULTS OF RAPE SURVEY

Characteristics of Victims

AGE: from 7 years to 39 years

under 15 years	8%
15–16 years	20%
17–18 years	23%
19–20 years	22%
21–22 years	10%
23–24 years	5%
25–26 years	5%
27 years or older	7%

HEIGHT:

under 5′1″	2%
5′1″–5′2″	12%
5′3″–5′4″	31%
5′5″–5′6″	37%
5′7″–5′8″	15%
5′9″ and over	3%

WEIGHT:

100–109 lbs.	8%
110–119 lbs.	16%
120–129 lbs.	32%
130–139 lbs.	25%
140–149 lbs.	6%
150 lbs. or over	9%
not known	4%

OCCUPATION:

student	57%
white collar	10%
blue collar	3%
teacher	5%
other	10%
unemployed	13%
unanswered	2%

MARITAL STATUS:

single	87%
married	7%
divorced	2%
separated	2%
not known	2%

Characteristics of Attackers

AGE:		OCCUPATION:	
under 15 years	2%	student	18%
15–19 years	15%	white collar	12%
20–24 years	37%	blue collar	17%
25–29 years	13%	other	7%
30–34 years	18%	unemployed	8%
35–39 years	5%	not known	38%
40–49 years	3%		
over 50 years	4%	MARITAL STATUS:	
not known	3%	single	38%
		married	18%
HEIGHT:		separated	2%
5'4"–5'6"	12%	divorced	7%
5'7"–5'9"	31%	widowed	2%
5'10"–6'	41%	not known	33%
over 6'	9%		
not known	7%		

WEIGHT:	
under 130 lbs.	1%
130–149 lbs.	16%
150–169 lbs.	33%
170–189 lbs.	31%
over 190 lbs.	12%
not known	7%

Characteristics of Attack

FAMILIARITY WITH ATTACKER:

not at all	33%
by sight	10%
acquaintance	37%
friend	3%
date	12%
relative	2%
ex-lover	3%
lover	0%

LOCATION OF ATTACK:

own home	24%
his home	23%
inside (other than own home or his home)	10%
street	8%
alley	5%
in car	18%
country	7%
park	5%

OTHER PEOPLE PRESENT AT TIME OF ATTACK:

yes	35%
no	65%

TIME OF ATTACK:

6 p.m.–8:59 p.m.	22%
9 p.m.–11:59 p.m.	26%
12 a.m.–2:59 a.m.	20%
3 a.m.–5:59 a.m.	10%
6 a.m.–8:59 a.m.	0%
9 a.m.–11:59 a.m.	2%
12 p.m.–2:59 p.m.	7%
3 p.m.–5:59 p.m.	13%

VICTIM FELT PERSUADED INTO A DANGEROUS SITUATION:

yes	43%
no	30%
not in control of situation	17%
not answered	10%

TYPE OF FORCE USED:

weapon	23%
beating	20%
choking	7%
hitting	23%
overpowering	73%
threat	38%

VICTIM ATTEMPTED TO RESIST ATTACK:

yes	82%
no	18%
How resisted:	
physically	82%
verbally	23%
screaming	14%

ATTITUDE OF RAPIST:
(Many of these attitudes appeared in combinations)

hostile	32%
contemptuous	28%
angry	22%
frightened	13%
matter-of-fact or calm	42%
righteous	22%

Aftermath

ATTACK REPORTED TO POLICE:
    yes 30%   (no 70%)
        Arrest resulted:
        yes 33%   (no 67%)
        Conviction resulted:
        yes 50%   (no 33%)
        pending 17%
        Rape conviction resulted:
        yes 17%

REACTION OF POLICE:
    sympathetic   38%
    unsympathetic   44%
    undetermined or
      unanswered   18%

LIFE AFFECTED:
    sexually   28%
    independence   27%
    fear of men   42%
    hostility toward men 17%
    self-respect   18%
    trust (in male-female
      relationship)   23%
    physical injuries   10%
    suicidal feelings   7%
    nightmares   5%

HELP RECEIVED FROM:
    friends   25%
    women's groups   12%
    professional counselors or
      ministers   8%
    relative   3%
    hospital   2%
    no help received   50%

REFLECTIONS ON ORGANIZING
ANTI-RAPE GROUPS

If you are interested in forming a rape crisis telephone line, you will need a phone and a group of women who are willing to train themselves and who are able, if necessary, to work at night, when they will be most needed. It is best, probably, to get a phone in a women's center, or an existing crisis intervention center. Regardless of what you name your group, be sure your telephone number is listed under Rape. Unless you are a lot richer than most groups of women, you will need all your money for other things, not for paying high rent on an office. Then you will have to investigate the hospitals and police which rape victims will have to deal with in your area. You will find some hospitals where the treatment is so bad that you will want to warn women not to go to them under any circumstances. Others may require great diligence on the part of the victim or the woman who goes with her. Eventually, you may be able to find one or two hospitals which are decent and refer women only to those. If your town has only one or two hospitals, you will simply have to fight it out with them until they provide the sort of treatment necessary.

You should build up a file of special resources. For example, some women who have been raped may need more help with the psychological and emotional trauma than your relatively untrained counselors can give them. You should be able to refer these women to a competent, feminist psychologist. And, if a woman cannot afford large fees, you should try to refer her to someone who will charge her on a sliding scale or to a clinic. You should also have the names of good women gynecologists. Sometimes a rape victim will have injuries that were not treated in the emergency room of the hospital where she was examined or she may need menstrual extraction if there is a possibility of pregnancy. Other women, who do not want to report to the police, may prefer to have the initial examination done by a private doctor. A good woman doctor can also be useful if the woman contracted a venereal disease and does not want to deal with a public VD clinic.

There will be other problems, arising from your particular situation, to be resolved. You are going to have to find out if you can expect cooperation from the police. And if you want it. Some groups, particularly in smaller cities and towns, have found that they are able to deal with the police. They may not discover a very high level of consciousness about women, but they find sympathy and a desire to cooperate in the ranks of their local police force. Other groups have decided to remain more independent. In Chicago, for example, the crisis lines made early tentative overtures to the police and were met with attitudes ranging from indifference to condescension to defensiveness. They decided to operate the lines without police cooperation. Later an ordinance was introduced in a city council meeting providing for an all-woman investigating team for rape; the lines of communication between the women and the police establishment were then, to some small extent, reopened. There may be some cooperation in the future, but it is only a possibility. In other cities, women have chosen to reject that possibility and, on principle, remain entirely independent of the police.

When pressing for a better rate of arrest and conviction, it is very important to remember that, in this country, rape and racism are too closely intertwined to deal with one without the other. In many states the rape laws have been used almost exclusively to keep black men away from white women. This is a fact and one which must be faced when asking for more and better prosecution. Your demand may be answered only by more prosecution and conviction of black men. We would not, of course, suggest that black rapists should not be convicted. We simply warn against allowing your anti-rape group to be used as a tool of the racist and "law and order" forces at work in our society.

Finally, there is a very difficult aspect of this work that no crisis line can ignore, publicity. The telephone number must be kept before the public. The line is of no value unless a woman who needs it knows where to find it. Crisis line organizers, therefore, often find themselves spending an enormous amount of time appearing on local talk shows, being interviewed by newspapers, and talking to groups who are able to help them publicize the number. The largest part of their money may be spent on stickers, leaflets, and posters (and, in some cases, even radio and television spots) featuring THE NUMBER. The women in the group become constantly aware of possibilities for mentioning the number.

Still, in the beginning, the women who staff the line may find that they are sitting for hours by the telephone, days and possibly weeks on end, with no calls. Unfortunately, this is not because the crisis line is not needed, but because it is not known. When the first calls come in, they will probably be from women who heard of the number some time after they were raped. Most of them will no longer have the option of reporting and prosecuting their cases because too much time has passed. These are women who want to talk to someone about the experience. So, for the first few months, your function on the line may be primarily a counseling one. This is not to be seen as in any way insignificant. Talking to rape victims is one of the most important things you will do as a member of a crisis line. And one of the most difficult.

It is important that the women who staff a crisis line be able to give technical advice, but it is even more important that their own consciousness about rape be high. One woman we talked to reported her shock when, on a speaking engagement, one of the new members of her crisis line launched into a tirade about how "sick and crazy" rapists are. In that situation, misinformation can be corrected and is only momentarily embarrassing. If the same woman had been on the line talking to a rape victim, the problem would have been serious. It is tempting to assume that any woman who is aware enough to want to work with the crisis line will be dependable. It is much more realistic to require that women who will be in a counseling position participate in consciousness-raising sessions regularly.

Here we run in to a primary problem of crisis lines: the emotional health of their members. Listening to women talk about being raped is painful. We found this out working on the book. Crisis line members find it difficult to work on the lines. There are ways of making this emotional drain more manageable, and crisis lines should try to be aware of these.

For example, the group should be careful about the number of hours any one woman spends on the line. If a group is having staffing problems and one of its members has a lot of free time and dedication, it may be tempting to schedule that woman as often as she wants to work. Yielding to that temptation can mean that in a few months you have one less member of your group. Unless done in moderation, staffing the line can exhaust a woman's emotional resources and cause serious problems. We do not need martyrs to the cause.

All of the members are likely to suffer from some kind of obsession with their personal security. A close friend of ours found herself involved more deeply than she had intended in a love affair because she could no longer stay in her apartment by herself. She would come home after hearing a woman relate how she had been raped by a man who broke into her apartment, and no number of locks could make her feel safe. Her rap group had to give her a training course on how to get to sleep in an empty apartment: night lights, music, sleeping in the living room. Finally, she was able to go to sleep alone with a lock on her bedroom door and a can of Mace by her bed. Other women have found that they simply cannot live by themselves. Paranoia is a legitimate problem, and one that should be recognized and talked about.

It is crucial that the members of a rape crisis line deal with each other with as much care as they give to the women who call them. A woman needs a lot of emotional support to be able to remain stable when dealing often with rape victims, and that support must come from others in the group.

It is also necessary to work on another front. Society must be forced to recognize its complicity in the crime of rape. To do this, rape must become a public issue. It must be talked about, written about, and thought about. The possibilities for raising your community's awareness of rape are limited only by your imagination and your judgment. Here are some suggestions about how to begin.

Any group that is going to undertake public re-education must begin with itself. Study groups using all the available material on the subject and exploring the personal experiences of the members make for a good foundation. One good technique is to ask all the women who will be participating to write down questions they have about rape, and then to try to answer them as a group. These questions will also come in handy when you prepare yourselves for speaking engagements.

When you feel that you're ready, start soliciting speaking dates from any and all groups in your area which have women members. That includes PTA's, church groups, high schools. The Chicago Women Against Rape group has talked to such diverse organizations as the Chicago Policemen's Wives' Association, Parents without Partners, a Catholic girls' school, and freshman orientation at a nearby university.

The primary purpose of this kind of speaking is to raise the level of consciousness of the individuals in the group, but it isn't a bad idea to have an answer to the question "What can we do about it?" just in case they ask. For example, you can recommend to a PTA meeting that they look for a good self-defense teacher and demand of their board of education that the young women in their schools be given self-defense training. Be careful when you make such suggestions, however, that it is clear that whatever project they might undertake will be only a beginning.

Besides personal speaking engagements—which, by the way, should be done by two or more women, unless you have some very experienced speakers—you can try to interest the women journalists in your town to do a feature article on rape for the women's page of your local newspaper. Many newspapers are trying to make their women's sections more relevant, and rape is certainly a subject of interest to all women. Such an article or series of articles can do a great deal to arouse public awareness, after which your group should be ready to make the next move.

Good luck.

RAPE CRISIS CENTERS AND OTHER ANTI-RAPE GROUPS

The following is a partial list of rape crisis centers and groups specifically interested in the problem of rape. Some of the centers have only a telephone listing. If you are interested in starting your own center, or if you want to find out about new centers that are opening, get in touch with the Rape Crisis Center Newsletter, P.O. Box 21005, Washington, D.C. 20009. Your local National Organization for Women (NOW) office will also be able to give you information on anti-rape activities in your community.

ALBUQUERQUE RAPE CRISIS CENTER, c/o The Women's Center, 824 Las Lomas N.E., Albuquerque, New Mexico 87106 (505) 277–3393

ANN ARBOR WOMEN'S CRISIS CENTER, 306 N. Division Street, Ann Arbor, Michigan 48108 (313) 761–WISE

BALTIMORE RAPE CRISIS CENTER (301) 366–6475

BAY AREA WOMEN AGAINST RAPE, P.O. Box 240, Berkeley, California 94701 (415) 845–RAPE

BOSTON AREA RAPE CRISIS CENTER, Cambridge, Massachusetts (617) 492–RAPE

CHAPEL HILL RAPE CRISIS CENTER, c/o Switchboard, 408 Rosemary Street, Chapel Hill, North Carolina (919) 929–7177

CHICAGO LEGAL ACTION FOR WOMEN, c/o Loop YWCA, 37 South Wabash, Chicago, Illinois 60603

CHICAGO RAPE CRISIS CENTER (312) 728–1920

CHICAGO WOMEN AGAINST RAPE, c/o Loop YWCA, 37 South Wabash, Chicago, Illinois 60603

COLUMBUS RAPE CRISIS CENTER, c/o Women Against Rape, P.O. Box 4442, Trivillage Station, Columbus, Ohio 43212 (614) 221–4447

DALLAS RAPE CRISIS LINE, c/o Women Against Rape, P.O. Box 12701, Dallas, Texas 75225 (214) 341–9400

DELAWARE RAPE CRISIS CENTER, Wilmington, Delaware (302) 998–2580

DENVER CRISIS LINE, c/o South East Neighborhood Services Bureau, 227 Clayton Street, Denver, Colorado 80206 (303) 321–8191

DETROIT WOMEN AGAINST RAPE, 18121 Patton, Detroit, Michigan 48219

IOWA CITY HOTLINE, c/o The Women's Center, 3 East Market Street, Iowa City, Iowa 52240 (319) 338–4800

LOS ANGELES RAPE CRISIS CENTER, 235 Hill Street, Santa Monica, California (213) 653–6333

MADISON RAPE CRISIS CENTER, P.O. Box 1312, Madison, Wisconsin 53701 (608) 251–RAPE

MEMPHIS CRISIS LINE, c/o People Against Rape, P.O. Box 12224, Memphis, Tennessee 38112 (615) CRISIS–3

MILWAUKEE WOMEN'S CRISIS LINE, c/o Women's Coalition, 2211 East Kenwood Blvd., Milwaukee, Wisconsin 53211 (414) 964–7535

MINNEAPOLIS RAPE CRISIS CENTER (612) 374–4357

NASHVILLE RAPE PREVENTION AND CRISIS CENTER, P.O. Box 12531, Acklen Station, Nashville, Tennessee 37212 (615) 297–9587

NEW JERSEY TASK FORCE AGAINST RAPE, Box 2163, Princeton, New Jersey 08540

NEW YORK WOMEN AGAINST RAPE, c/o The Women's Center, 243 West 20th Street, New York, New York (212) 675–7720

OKLAHOMA CITY RAPE CRISIS CENTER, c/o YWCA, 320 Park Avenue, Oklahoma City, Oklahoma 73102 (405) 232–7688

PHILADELPHIA WOMEN ORGANIZED AGAINST RAPE, Box 17374, Philadelphia, Pennsylvania 19105 (215) 823–7997

ROANOKE RAPE CRISIS LINE, 3515 Williamson Road, Roanoke, Virginia 24012 (703) 366–6030

ST. LOUIS, MISSOURI, RAPE CENTER (314) 727–2727

SAN DIEGO RAPE CRISIS CENTER (714) 239–RAPE

SAN JOSE WOMEN AGAINST RAPE, 9th and Carlos Streets, San Jose, California 95192 (408) 287–3000

SEATTLE RAPE RELIEF (206) 632–4795

WASHINGTON, D.C., RAPE CRISIS CENTER, P.O. Box 21005, Washington, D.C. 20009 (202) 333–RAPE

ADDITIONAL LISTINGS OF
RAPE CRISIS CENTERS

As this book was going to press, we learned of several more rape crisis centers now operating:

CAMDEN WOMEN AGAINST RAPE, c/o Contact, Camden, New Jersey (609) 667–3000

DAYTON WOMEN AGAINST RAPE COLLECTIVE, Women's Center, 1309 North Main Street, Dayton, Ohio 45405 (513) 223–2462

DETROIT RAPE CRISIS LINE, P.O. Box 35271, Seven Oaks Station, Detroit, Michigan (313) 832–RAPE

EUGENE RAPE CRISIS CENTER, P.O. Box 562, Eugene, Oregon 97401 (503) 343–9986

FRESNO RAPE COUNSELLING SERVICE, P.O. Box 708, Clovis, California 93612 (209) 222–RAPE

GAINESVILLE RAPE CRISIS CENTER, P.O. Box 12888, Gainesville, Florida 32604 (904) 377–RAPE

GRAND RAPIDS RAPE CRISIS TEAM, Box 6161, Station C, Grand Rapids, Michigan 49506 (616) 456–3535

JACKSONVILLE WOMEN'S RAPE CRISIS CENTER, Jacksonville, Florida (904) 384–6488

KALAMAZOO RAPE CRISIS CENTER, Kalamazoo, Michigan (616) 345–3036

MACON RAPE CRISIS LINE, c/o The Woman's Center, Macon, Georgia (912) 742–8661

MARIN RAPE CRISIS CENTER, P.O. Box 823, Kentfield, California 94904 (415) 453–8114

MIAMI RAPE TREATMENT CENTER, c/o Jackson Memorial Hospital, Miami, Florida (305) 325–RAPE

NEW HAVEN RAPE CRISIS CENTER (203) 397–2273

OMAHA RAPE ADVISORS, Omaha, Nebraska (402) 345–RAPE

PORTLAND RAPE RELIEF HOTLINE, Portland, Oregon (503) 235–5333

SAN ANTONIO RAPE CRISIS LINE, P.O. Box 28061, San Antonio, Texas 78228 (512) 433–1251

SAN BERNADINO RAPE CRISIS SERVICE, c/o Family Service Agency, 1669 E Street, San Bernadino, California (714) 886–4889

SPRINGFIELD RAPE CRISIS CENTER, Room 212, 292 Worthington Street, Springfield, Massachusetts 01003 (413) 737–RAPE

WESTPORT PEOPLE AGAINST RAPE, 27 Reichert Circle, Westport, Connecticut 06880 (203) 576–0397

YPSILANTI RAPE RELIEF, Ypsilanti, Michigan (313) 485–3222

Bibliography

* Amir, Menachim, *Patterns in Forcible Rape*. Chicago and London, University of Chicago Press, 1971.

"Code R for Rape." *Newsweek,* 80 (November 13, 1972), p. 75.

† "Defending Yourself Against Rape; excerpts from *Our Bodies, Ourselves." Ladies' Home Journal,* 90 (July 1973), p. 62.

De Gramont, S., and de Gramont, N. R., "Couple-Speak Rape, True and False." *Vogue,* 157 (June 1971), pp. 108–9.

Gebhard, Paul, "1965 Kinsey Report." *Ladies' Home Journal* (May 1965), p. 121.

‡ Griffin, Susan, "Rape: The All-American Crime." *Ramparts Magazine,* 10 (September 1971), pp. 26–35.

Hayman, Charles R., M.D.; Lanza, Charlene, R. N.; and Fuentes, Roberto, B.A., "Rape in the District of Columbia." Paper presented to the convention of the American Public Health Association, October 1971.

"Healthy Rise in Rape." *Newsweek,* 80 (July 31, 1972), p. 72.

§ Herschberger, Ruth, *Adam's Rib*. New York, Harper & Row, 1970.

Lake, A., "Rape: The Unmentionable Crime." *Good Housekeeping* (November 1971), pp. 104–5.

Lear, M. W., "Q. If You Rape a Woman and Steal Her TV, What Can They Get You For in N.Y.? A. Stealing Her TV." *The New York Times Magazine,* January 30, 1972: Discussion, February 27, 1972.

Lear, M. W., "What Can You Say about Laws That Tell a Man: If You Rob a Woman, You Might as Well Rape Her Too—the Rape Is Free?" *Redbook,* 139 (September 1972), p. 83.

"Least Punished Crime." *Newsweek,* 80 (December 18, 1972), p. 33.

Lipton, M. A., "Violence Is a Part of the Times." *U.S. News and World Report,* 70 (January 25, 1971), pp. 73–4.

Loenig, R., "Rape: Most Rapidly Increasing Crime." *McCalls,* 100 (July 1973), p. 25.

|| McDonald, John Marshall, *Rape: Offenders and Their Victims.* Springfield, Illinois, Charles C. Thomas, 1971.

Menen, A., "Rapes of Bangla Desh." *The New York Times Magazine* (July 23, 1972), p. 10.

"Portrait of a Rapist." *Newsweek,* 82 (August 20, 1973), p. 67.

"Rape." *Encyclopaedia Britannica,* 1969 ed., Vol. 22, p. 981.

"Rape Wave: Creation of Rape Investigation and Analysis Section." *Newsweek,* 81 (January 29, 1973), p. 59.

Schultz, Terri, "Rape, Fear, and the Law." *The Chicago Guide* (November 1972), pp. 56–62.

"Sex Offenses and Sex Offenders." *The Annals of the American Academy* (March 1969), pp. 151–2.

Shultz, Gladys, "Society and the Sex Criminal." *The Reader's Digest,* (November 1966), pp. 141–6.

Southerland, Sandra, M.S.S.A., and Scherl, Donald J., M.D., "Patterns of Response among Victims of Rape." *Journal of Orthopsychiatry,* 40:3 (April 1970).

Women Against Rape, *Stop Rape.* Privately printed in Detroit, 1971.

"Women Against Rape." *Time,* 101 (April 23, 1973), p. 104.

* One of the few sources of statistical material, this book is sexist in the extreme (e.g., victims as well as rapists are referred to as participants in the crime). The number of outright errors in the tabulation and presentation of statistics indicates that the book may never have been copy-edited. Also, the conclusions that Amir draws from his data often have little or no relation to the data themselves.

† Very good.

‡ This is one of the first and certainly one of the most important articles ever written on the subject of rape as a political crime, that is, a crime against women. We owe a great deal to Griffin's thought.

§ Herschberger's contribution to thinking about rape cannot be overestimated. Besides, the entire book, first published in the thirties, is a delight to read. A necessity for the overworked, overwrought feminist.

|| A singularly offensive, semiacademic book, full of case histories that read like cheap detective-magazine pieces. At times Mr. McDonald reaches astounding conclusions from inconclusive facts; he tries to demonstrate the injustice of statutory rape by citing a case in which a male adult was convicted of threatening and overpowering a thirteen-year-old girl in spite of her questionable reputation—she admitted that she had kissed the man previously. The book is currently (and deservedly) out of print.